Completing the Computer Puzzle

A Guide for Early Childhood Educators

Suzanne Thouvenelle
MOBIUS Corporation and
Johns Hopkins University, Faculty Associate

Cynthia J. Bewick
Tri-County Head Start in Paw Paw, MI

Boston   New York   San Francisco
Mexico City   Montreal   Toronto   London   Madrid   Munich   Paris
Hong Kong   Singapore   Tokyo   Cape Town   Sydney

MT

Series Editor: Traci Mueller
Editorial Assistant: Erica Tromblay
Senior Marketing Manager: Elizabeth Fogarty
Editorial-Production Administrator: Anna Socrates
Editorial-Production Service: Omegatype Typography, Inc.
Manufacturing Buyer: Andrew Turso
Composition Buyer: Linda Cox
Cover Administrator: Kristina Mose-Libon
Electronic Composition: Omegatype Typography, Inc.
Text Designer: Glenna Collett

For related titles and support materials, visit our online catalog at www.ablongman.com.

Library of Congress Cataloging-in-Publication Data

Thouvenelle, Suzanne.
   Completing the computer puzzle : a guide for early childhood educators / Suzanne Thouvenelle, Cynthia J. Bewick.
       p. cm.
   Includes bibliographical references and index.
   ISBN 0-205-26544-8
     1. Early childhood education—Computer-assisted instruction.   2. Computers and children.   3. Educational technology.   I. Bewick, Cynthia J.   II. Title.

LB1139.35.C64 T46 2003
371.33'4—dc21

2002026242

Printed in the United States of America

10   9   8   7   6   5   4   3   2   07   06

3/4/08

Brief Contents

Contents

Chapter **3**   **Selecting Hardware**   41

Chapter **6**   **Involving Parents: The Home/School Connection**   116

Chapter **7**   **Confronting Common Myths**   134

Chapter **8** **Exploring the Internet: What, Why, and How** 145

Preface

Today's children are bombarded by technology. They use it for play, for learning, and for communication. They experience it at home. Sometimes very young children are introduced to computers before they begin formal schooling. Technology is also assuming a greater importance in schools. However, the answer to the question "What is the effectiveness of technology in instruction?" remains elusive. We educators tend to be optimistic about the value of educational technology, yet we often act based on incomplete information.

Countless children spend extended periods daily with computers and other technology-based devices. Yet we do not know exactly how technology affects children's cognitive, social, emotional, and physical development. There are large gaps in published literature in all these areas. Small sample size and limited research designs are characteristic of studies that involve young children. Little research has focused on the impact of computers in classrooms of young children, those between the ages of 3 and 8 years old.

Most of the research on children and computers focuses on older students and their use of computers in schools and, therefore, deals with cognitive and academic performance. For example, one of the most extensive national studies of computer use to date was conducted by Educational Testing Services (Wenglinsky, 1998), reporting on fourth- and eighth-grade students' academic and educational uses of computers. The ETS study showed that students who spent time on computers with drill software actually scored worse on math tests than students who spent no time with computers. Wenglinsky suggests that these lower test scores are caused by the ineffective but widespread use of computers for repetitive drills, instead of simulations and real-life applications of math concepts, which are more effective.

Some who began as advocates of computer technology in schools have reconsidered the prospects. Jane Healy (2000) observed that current computer use in primary education did not live up to its promise. She noted that although teachers had computers in their classrooms, they made little effort to link children's computer use with the curriculum. Computers were most frequently used to reward students who had completed their "work" or to mollify students who had behavior problems. She faults both the lack of professional development for teachers and the inadequate quality of available software.

As yet there is no clear research-based evidence to support the notion that children will miss something vital for future school success if they do not access computers early and often. Yet public perception that computer use is positive dominates the news, especially when we consider the "digital divide" between rich and poor, where we often read of low-income parents demanding more access to computers for their children. Available research does not yet compel us to insist that classroom computers be mandated—like immunizations.

In spite of the lack of definitive research, and in spite of lingering questions from some knowledgeable professionals, in this book we take a position encouraging teachers to use computers in classrooms with young children. In the last decade we have visited hundreds of classrooms in which teachers used technology with young children, and we have often observed outstanding use of the technology. We are confident that in time the formal research studies will document these exciting events. Our goal is to tell you some of what we have observed and learned to help you adopt the effective practices and avoid the ineffective practices.

We recommend beginning with strategies for using classroom computers based on the promising practices that we do know to date. For example:

- Choose quality software that helps teachers and children use the computer as a tool for learning.
- Select software that meets the needs of *all* children to explore, discover, create, and communicate, including those with special learning requirements and home languages other than English.
- Locate computers within the early childhood classroom and set up the center just as you would any other learning area.
- Link computer experiences with other hands-on activities to promote knowledge construction and deepen understanding of concepts.
- Demonstrate the use of computers as a tool so young children have opportunities to observe adult role models.
- Provide professional development for staff in terms of hands-on computer workshops and ongoing support for educators.
- Set aside time for teachers to practice and gain confidence in using computers and then provide specific meetings at which they can share their experiences using classroom computers.

These documented strategies support reasoned and practical use of information technology, specifically classroom computers. Computers are no different from any other media or method, both in their great potential to help children learn, as well as in their potential for misuse.

We believe a balanced use of computers can be effective for young children. Only when early childhood educators accept the challenge of learning how to integrate computers into their classrooms, through thoughtful software selection and creative use with children, will we begin to develop a base of effective professional practice. Educators can advance everyone's knowledge by documenting and sharing their own successful technology practices. This foundation of effective technology use can extend the benefits to other educators and children as they use computers to actively support the learning process.

Why This Book?

Computers have been used with young children in classrooms for more than a decade and a half, and teachers across the nation have learned much about the best ways to effectively integrate computers into their classrooms. The purpose of this book is to organize and summarize the most important things we have learned so you can benefit from them as well.

We responded to the challenges of learning about computer use with young children by asking questions. In a major formative evaluation of computer use in preschool classrooms (MOBIUS, 1994) we asked questions about hardware, software, children's responses, the classroom environment, staff development opportunities, and parent involvement. Since the early 1990s, we have actively explored issues surrounding the introduction and use of information technology with young children, primarily from a practitioner perspective.

In addition to conducting this study and reviewing available research and current literature, we have gone directly to teachers. We talked with thousands of teachers in their classrooms and in various types of educational workshops and training seminars. They asked us question after question during professional conferences and seminars. We were able to sort many of these questions into categories based on similar topics. Specific areas of inquiry emerged.

The methods we used were simple and straightforward. At regional and national Head Start and early childhood education conferences we asked workshop participants, "What three things do you want to know about computer use with young children?" Participants jotted down and submitted their questions. Some of you may have even attended those workshops.

These questions, organized by category (e.g., hardware, software, curriculum, costs), became the content of the workshop. The authors and the participants shared experiences as they collaborated in responding to these questions. We recorded the questions and responses, and the chapters in this book are the result of this process. It's been more than ten years since the first such workshop was conducted, and yet even today we find that educators continue to have similar questions. Responses to these questions are tied to the National Association for the Education of Young Children (NAEYC) Technology Position Statement, to the Administration for Children and Families (ACF) and Title 1 Performance Standards, and to related guidance on developmentally appropriate computer use.

Grounding the chapter discussion in principles of child development and referencing NAEYC and ACF guidance should assist early childhood educators who remain concerned about the implications of computer use with young children. For these concerned educators, chapter discussions should foster movement (at least cognitively) toward considering or adopting a balanced and effective use of classroom computers. Think about computers as a tool, like crayons or pencils. Computers are *not* the center of the activity; they fade into and become part of the fabric of the many engaging classroom activities that help children learn. For educators who are experienced computer users, the chapter discussions should reinforce, support, and extend your effective use of classroom computers.

Who Is Our Audience?

We wrote this book both for beginning teachers and for experienced teachers new to technology. So for you "newbies," get ready for an adventure! For others, this book can help you use computers effectively with young children regardless of your experience. You may feel you don't have the expertise to decide whether computers can benefit your program or to select quality software for young learners. You may be a seasoned Head Start teacher who has just received a new classroom computer. Perhaps you're studying early childhood education and wondering how computers that are so mechanistic and so often used for drill can support young children's creativity. You might even be an experienced kindergarten teacher who has used computers for several years but wants to connect computers more closely to your curriculum. You may work with preschoolers in a child care center or with primary grade children in a public school. If you teach (or plan to teach) children between 3 and 8 years old, and use computers with them, we think you will find this book helpful.

We hope to help preservice and in-service educators share the excitement of an innovation in education. Using computers with appropriate software and strong ties to a sound curriculum can enhance and enrich young children's learning and promote their achievement. Computers offer unique opportunities for collaboration, problem solving, and self-expression. Realizing the potential of the technology can pose serious demands on teachers' time, effort, and commitment.

We designed this book to help you consider these issues and create experiences that encourage children's active learning in a technological age. We want to help you jump-start your journey on the road to self-sufficiency with computers. In this spirit we chose to avoid complicated technical language and instead offer clear, straightforward explanations of concepts. We base our discussions and descriptions on real-life experiences and classroom examples. Charts, photos, illustrations, and diagrams help convey the information and promote synthesis of knowledge.

How Is the Book Organized?

Near the beginning of each chapter you'll see a "Teachers Ask" section presenting the questions we heard most frequently from early childhood teachers with a brief response to each question. Next, we summarize what you'll know after reading the chapter. Throughout each chapter you'll notice "Consider this . . ." boxes that connect a specific statement from the NAEYC Technology Position Statement with a recommended practice related to using classroom computers. Finally, each chapter offers a set of activities designed to give you a chance to apply what was covered in the text. These will encourage you to think about and apply the concepts and classroom practices you've read about. These activities are designed to help you become an active player in the computer age. Always remember that the *teacher is key* to effective and meaningful educational uses of classroom computers.

Each chapter in this book explores an essential piece of the classroom computer puzzle. Chapter 1 presents the premise that the teacher is key. The role and responsibility of the teacher as instructional leader are discussed in the context of the decision to acquire and effectively use technology in prekindergarten and primary grade classrooms. Understanding the nature of classroom computers as an innovation with great potential is balanced with the need for thoughtful decision making on the part of the teacher.

Chapter 2, "Choosing Quality Software," emphasizes the point that simply getting computers into the classroom is not the end of the journey. Careful review of software highlights the need to be aware of implicit messages communicated. The only way the potential and positive impact of classroom computers can be realized is by selecting software applications that are consistent with the principles of teaching for understanding.

Chapter 3, "Selecting Hardware," tackles the next piece of the classroom computer puzzle. Simple descriptions of computer system components and the technical details of hardware selection are offered.

Chapter 4, "Setting Up and Introducing the Classroom Computer," explicitly describes how to organize the computer system components. The discussion includes examples of effective management strategies that ensure equity of access to computers. Successful techniques for introducing computers to young children are described.

Chapter 5, "Linking Computers with Curriculum and Assessment," explores principles and issues surrounding technology, early education curriculum, and assessment. How can software be used most effectively with young children? What kinds of software and classroom activities promote brain-based learning and neural branching? How can technology help teachers enhance their curriculum and assessment process?

Chapter 6, "Involving Parents: The Home/School Connection," looks at how parents and family members fit in with technology initiatives in early education. This chapter provides suggestions for safe Internet use and describes ways that other teachers are using computers to effectively link with parents and families.

Chapter 7, "Confronting Common Myths," helps you examine your own biases toward information technology. Compare your misperceptions about information technology with the commonly held beliefs of others. Find out how these myths affect your attitudes toward classroom computer use with young children.

Chapter 8, "Exploring the Internet: What, Why, and How," helps separate fact from fantasy and encourages educators to thoughtfully consider Internet use with young children. Together we explore how the Internet can be used effectively within the early childhood environment and underscore the need for safeguards and privacy.

Acknowledgments

Books do not write themselves. They are the result of collaborative efforts that involve individuals beyond those who are designated as the authors. This book is no exception. We appreciate all the early childhood educators who contributed their questions, ideas, and encouragement. In particular, we acknowledge with gratitude: the management staff at Tri-County Head Start in Paw Paw, Michigan, who endorsed and supported our efforts and the teachers who endured several interruptions for photos of them and their students using computers; our colleagues at MOBIUS for their insight, creativity, and endless ways to rethink problems; and finally, every teacher who attended one of our NAEYC or NHSA workshops, or our hands-on computer sessions, and talked with us about using classroom computers. We thank each of you. We would also like to thank the following reviewers: Sharon Milburn, California State Fullerton; Susan Paintal, California State University; and Linda Pickett, University of North Florida.

About the Authors

Suzanne Thouvenelle

Dr. Thouvenelle is the director of research and development at MOBIUS Corporation in Alexandria, Virginia. She is actively investigating classroom computer use in early education settings including preschool and the primary grades. For the past thirty years Dr. Thouvenelle has taught students from preschool to graduate school, directed federally funded research and program evaluation projects, developed software and curriculum materials, and served on the faculty of several universities. She collaborated with colleagues to write the NAEYC Position Statements on Technology and Young Children.

Cynthia J. Bewick

Dr. Bewick is currently the education services manager for Tri-County Head Start in Paw Paw, Michigan. She has an extensive and varied background that includes managing and supervising in early education programs. For more than twenty-five years she has actively pursued her interests in young children, curriculum, and teacher preparation. She has taught university and community college courses in administration of child care programs, curriculum and instruction, human development, and educational psychology.

The Teacher Is Key

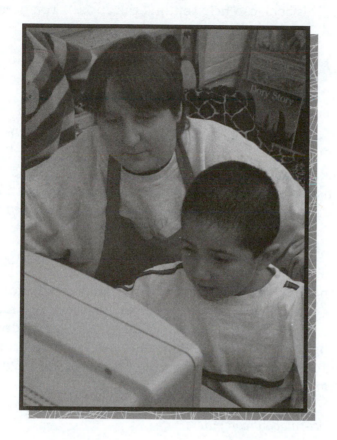

Whether you are a fearless innovator or computer skeptic, few dispute the presence of computers in our society today. Some of us must have our cellular telephones or handheld computers nearby in our pockets, brief-cases, or automobiles. Information, communication, and every conceivable shopping item are easily available with just a few mouse clicks through the Internet. Even if you prefer direct contact with a living, breathing person, it is likely that a computer affects your daily life from your credit card accounts, medical records, grocery store purchases, and electric bill to your overdue library books.

Although Americans at all income levels are increasingly connecting to the Internet, certain groups are less likely to have computers at home. In particular, substantially fewer African American and Hispanic families use home computers than other groups (NTIA, 2000). Some suggest that early childhood programs, schools, and libraries become sources for computer access as children prepare for technology-based work environments (Day & Yarbrough, 1998; NTIA, 2000; Taylor, 2000).

As the classroom teacher, you can be the key to your children's future success with computers. By providing appropriate and integrated computer experiences, you help children understand how to use computers as tools for learning. This book can help you find the answers you need.

 ## Q & A 🕸 Teachers Ask

▶ *Why are some teachers reluctant to use computers with young children?*

Researchers suggest several common reasons (Bilton, 1996; Lemke & Coughlin, 1998; Sheingold & Hadley, 1990; Wood, Willoughby, & Specht, 1998). Think of each of these reasons as a missing piece of the puzzle. These reasons include lack of confidence, inexperience with computers, inadequate training and planning, and lack of computers and curriculum guidelines.

▶ *Why should I use computers?*

You provide not only the instruction and skill children need for using computers as a tool but also the access to computers that some may not have at home. As the teacher, you are the children's strongest advocate. With your knowledge, experience, and leadership you ensure that computers are integrated into the curriculum appropriately and used in ways that enhance children's learning.

▶ *How can I learn about computers?*

You have a number of options depending on the educational opportunities in your local community and your own motivation. No matter what option you choose, it is critical that you actually "mess about" with computers and talk with others about what you learn (Bewick, 2000).

▶ *Where do I begin?*

First, complete a self-assessment inventory of your attitudes, skills, and experience with computers, in general, and with young children, in particular. Then plan your personal next steps toward gaining greater knowledge and competency with computers. Finally, identify important stakeholders so you can make collaborative plans for using computers with children.

After Reading This Chapter, You'll Know

- Characteristics of teachers who are effective computer users.
- How to assess important issues related to your computer readiness.
- Your personal next steps.
- Who your important stakeholders are.

Why Teachers Are the Key to Quality Computer Experiences for Young Children

Using computers with young children is not an isolated experience. You might mistakenly believe that as long as the computer works properly, everything else will work smoothly. However, the technology equation includes not only computer software and hardware but also teachers. The classroom environment and the broader program context also play important roles. Teachers and computers are part of the immediate classroom and broader program context in public school, child care, Head Start, and preschool. Therefore, teachers influence their environment and the environment influences teachers. For example, if you're a fan of using computers with children but your classroom doesn't have a sufficient number of electrical outlets, you've been affected by the environment. In the same fashion, even if you have a fabulous classroom computer center and lots of administrative support, but you have limited knowledge about computers, you're likely to influence this environment negatively through your beliefs and actions about computers.

The science of human ecology looks at this classroom situation and develops principles that define and describe these connections. Bronfenbrenner (1979) and Lerner (1984) identify "reciprocal interaction" between organisms (living things) and their environments as one of these human ecological principles. In addition to the family, preschool classrooms are one of the most influential microsystems in children's lives due to their potential effect on social and cognitive development (Barnett, 1995; Bronfenbrenner, 1979; Schweinhart, Barnes, & Weikart, 1993). When something related to the environment changes, it affects something else. This could be a social institution, other living things, or physical items. Lerner (1984, 1986) calls this process "dynamic contextualism." Teachers, computers, and their environment form a dynamic relationship. This relationship can impact the effective use of computers with children.

Figure 1.1 shows the relationships among teachers, computer hardware and software, the children, and the classroom environment. As the central

Figure 1.1 The "Dynamic Context" for Teaching and Learning with Computers

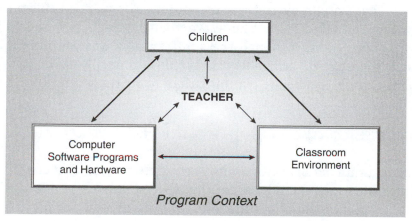

point of this figure, the teacher affects whatever occurs within or between these elements. This chapter focuses on the teacher's essential role in the technology equation. We believe that unless teachers recognize, assess, and plan according to their individual preferences, children will not receive the potential benefits of technology. Teachers serve as a model for their students through their attitudes toward and use of computers. Literally, the teacher is the key for unlocking the challenges of teaching and learning with computers. The teacher is the missing piece of the effective computer use puzzle.

4

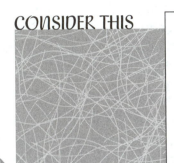

CONSIDER THIS

Teachers are professionals who determine whether computers are age appropriate, individually appropriate, and culturally appropriate for their group of children (NAEYC, 1996). Teachers consider and evaluate whether particular computer activities support children's development and learning. These decisions made by teachers can influence program quality.

Planning and Preparation Are Important *before* Using Computers with Children

We advocate young children using computers as long as the important pieces of the technology puzzle fit together. When one piece is missing, the puzzle is incomplete and important connections cannot occur. We want children and teachers to have positive experiences with technology. Too often we hear of computers that remain unpacked, or soon have missing and broken parts and remain unused because no one is there to help the teacher. This lack of support and techincal help prevents classroom staff from gaining a comfort level with computers. Furthermore, it diminishes the potential educational benefit of an expensive resource.

Adequate planning and preparation can prevent these and other possible disasters, especially if the teacher is actively involved in the process. Sometimes this isn't the case and teachers are not part of the decision. For example, as one administrator enthusiastically described her "surprise" for the teachers (new classroom computers), one teacher innocently asked about the teaching staff. The administrator replied that none of the teachers knew she had purchased these computers. She planned this purchase as a great surprise but did not know whether the teachers were interested in having computers. Although the administrator was well intentioned, she made a costly and avoidable mistake. It is generally easier to prevent problems through deliberate planning than to fix them after they occur.

Professional Development Is Essential

There are a number of reasons why computers are not used effectively or well integrated into the school curriculum. Technology is not a primary focus of teacher preparation programs, schools, districts, or practitioners.

Only limited numbers of teacher educators model appropriate use of computers in the teaching/learning process with preservice or graduate-level teachers. Some school administrators (principals and directors) do not appear to have a deep understanding of technology applications. School districts don't have a vision of how to develop a technology infrastructure, especially when it comes to teacher support. Typically, a district's idea of integration is to put the responsibility in the hands of individual teachers and place a computer coordinator on campus and hope that computer integration occurs (McGee, 2000).

Initial formative research of computer use with Head Start and other early education programs identified teacher training and support as the single most important factor in successful computer use (MOBIUS, 1994). Since then other teacher educators and staff development specialists (Becker, 2000; Cuban, 1999; Hohmann, 1994) have emphasized this need. Bewick (2000) identified two additional factors that affect teacher use of classroom computers: (1) time to learn and practice software programs and (2) opportunities to share technology-related experiences with others.

Your appropriate use of computers and software is more than just getting them into the classroom. Obviously, you must first have these tools available. However, without adequate staff preparation and ongoing support, you could consider the entire expenditure a gross waste of time, money, and other early childhood resources. As the early childhood teacher, you must be able to participate in hands-on workshops with some opportunities for follow-up training. Wright and Thouvenelle (1991) recommend establishing a developmental perspective when working with teachers. This helps teachers support a child-centered approach to computer use.

A Developmental Perspective on Staff Development

Effective staff development strategies acknowledge that teachers have different levels of willingness to accept an innovation and different kinds of experience and skill with technology in general. A developmental approach means that teachers go through stages as the result of training, support, practice, and experience in actually using computers with their students. Computers are an innovation and any new educational practice, methodology, or curriculum requires at least three years before full acceptance and integration occur. This time frame is unfortunate because nearly every three years (or often much sooner), software and computers become obsolete. These changes challenge teachers to stay updated and may provide an excuse for those unwilling to take the technology plunge. Given this understanding of the needs of teachers and the state of hardware and software innovation and development, "one-shot" training is clearly inadequate.

In-service workshops need to focus on helping teachers gain a comfort level with technology as a first step in the process. After all, you might find it very difficult to even think about using a computer keyboard or mouse if anxiety inhibits your response. Wright and Thouvenelle (1991) recommend that teachers become active, hands-on learners by unpacking and

*S*taff development is a cornerstone of effective classroom computer use.

assembling the hardware (computer, cables, printer, monitor, etc.). This is a first step in the process of demystifying the information technology experience. You can control the concrete process of plugging in and connecting all the pieces in a computer learning center (and having it actually turn "on" when the power switch is activated) and reduce your anxiety. As you gain comfort and confidence with your newly acquired skills, you are also better able to troubleshoot problems with the computer center.

CONSIDER THIS

Appropriate technology is integrated into the regular learning environment and used as one of many options to support children's learning (NAEYC, 1996). The extent to which curriculum plans tie technology-related activities with literacy and other educational goals is a good indicator of successful integration.

Looking at What You Know and Think

As the teacher, you are responsible for whether children can and do use computers successfully and effectively. Through your actions and attitudes, you communicate just how you feel about computer technology, even if you never speak one word. This unspoken communication occurs regardless of whether you love computers or hate them.

Many of us who are early childhood educators generally prefer personal interactions rather than tinkering around with things. We tend to be "high touch" and "low tech." This may even be part of the reason why you chose a career working directly with young children. You may pride yourself on being responsive to young children's developing needs that they often communicate nonverbally. However, we don't often apply this same perceptive knowledge to machines or other technical things. Carefully consider your own personal characteristics and factors as you think about your role in using computers with children.

As an early childhood teacher, you must consider several personal issues in order to make a sensible decision about using computers with young children. We want you to avoid having your computer sit unused in a closet or covered with a sheet. Your attitudes and experiences, both with children as well as technology, the status of your classroom environment, and other program plans can and do affect what happens. Although you may believe computers are a great opportunity for your students, this belief does not guarantee you automatic success.

- Are you willing to look carefully at your own attitudes toward computers?
- Do you have any experience with computers?
- What do you believe about using computers with young children?
- Can you think about what you know now and what you need to learn next?
- Have you considered how your classroom or program environment might help or hinder your computer use with children?

You may discover that one area in particular needs attention. But wait, we're getting ahead of ourselves. Take a few minutes here and look at some issues that can affect how you successfully use computers with children.

Knowledge about Computers. If someone asked you, "Tell me everything you know about computers," what would you say? Could you easily talk about how you don't know if you could live without e-mail or use of your computer for word processing? Would you squirm a little and try to change the subject? Perhaps you don't know the answer to these questions. You probably know more than you think, but fear has created a giant barrier.

Early computer advocates insisted that each of us would have to learn complicated programming language and other related skills before we could become effective technology users. You may be someone who heard this message loud and clear. Listen carefully. This is *not true* for most people and their computer needs. Both software programs and computer hardware continue to become more "user friendly." Some manufacturers advertise their systems as "plug and play"—you unpack the computer, place it on your tabletop, and plug it in. Turn the on switch and "ta, da!" everything works. After the computer starts up, several software packages use small pictures or icons to tell you what button to push to get the results you want. Once you get in practice, the process is relatively easy.

Meanwhile, many people took the early computer users' message to the depths of their very soul. You might hear yourself say, "I'm going to break something" or "I know I'm going to mess this up" based on the residual effects that you cannot and do not have sufficient knowledge to operate a computer. When you have this perspective, you are likely to transfer these fears to your students.

Having gone through all of this, the bottom line is that you must have some basic computer knowledge. Early childhood educators perceived that this single factor was the most important ingredient for making computer use with children easier (Bewick, 2000). Learn basic computer operations, what to avoid, and some simple troubleshooting strategies. Stay away from anyone who preaches the virtues of sophisticated programming. You can become an effective user without this extensive knowledge base. How you learn basic computer skills and appropriate use with young children is another story. Keep reading.

Previous Experiences with Computers.   What has been the quality of your experiences with computers? If someone was shouting over your shoulder (or maybe it seemed like this) while you endured a giant list of "do nots," it is likely that you'd probably rather do anything else other than work with a computer. On the other hand, you might have been able to experiment with the process at your own pace. Perhaps you even had someone who acted as your "computer coach" (who was nonjudgmental in his or her feedback about your knowledge and skills) as you inched your way along.

We know from basic psychological principles that if your previous experiences with anything (or anyone for that matter) were negative, you are unlikely to repeat them, at least by choice. In the same vein, if your experiences make you feel successful, your anxiety level is substantially reduced the next time you engage in this activity. The goal is to balance your challenges with your level of frustration as you increase your competency.

Comfort Level with Computers.   As human beings, we tend to repeat those activities that make us feel comfortable and avoid those that cause tension. This is true with computers as well. You want to optimize your comfort level as much as you can. This may mean that you decide not to use computers this year with your students in order to allow yourself time to become comfortable with technology. Or you may begin integrating computers only in the literacy portion of your curriculum. On the other hand, if you are feeling more comfortable and confident, you may broaden the scope of your current computer curriculum. You may choose to take a formal Introduction to Computers course or request that you have a "computer coach" to help. Your coach could be anyone who has computer skills that are slightly more advanced than yours. (Did you notice that we didn't say that this coach needed to have a degree in engineering?) Just as children can learn from more experienced peers, so can you.

Using or Doing Something New and Different.   When was the last time you tried something different or brand new? Are you the person who has the latest gadget before anyone else even knows about it? Or do other people go to great lengths to convince you to try something before you actually try it out? Perhaps you chose to sit back and see how others cope with this new thing before you try it yourself.

Figure 1.2 Find Out What Kind of Star You Are

I'M THE FIRST!

If it's new, I want to try or buy it right now. I jump in immediately. I'm way in front of most everyone else.

VERY CAUTIOUS

I'm the last to try something new. I'm very cautious and skeptical about something new.

ASK ME HOW IT WORKS

If it is new, I investigate. I try it, usually before many people. Then others ask me for advice about how it works.

EVERYONE SAYS I SHOULD

I try new things after lots of other people tell me I should. I am somewhat cautious and skeptical.

I'M NOT THE FIRST OR THE LAST

I have a wait and see approach. I'm not the first or the last to try new things. You can describe me as steady and deliberate.

Some experts believe that people fall into different categories when using or adopting something new, including computers. Although these new activities may not be new to others, the researchers consider them as innovations when they are new to that individual. As your educational level and the variety and range of your social relationships increase, the more likely you are to try an innovation before other people (Cory, 1983; Hall & Loucks, 1977; Moersch, 1995; Rogers, 1995).

Does this mean you must return to school or begin meeting several new people? Not exactly. Is it better to be first or even last? Although it may seem so at times, using computers is not a race. We bring up these points so that you can identify your own tendencies and preferences. All categories of learners have unique strengths. Can you imagine if every person bought all the new technological computer gizmos as soon as they came out? You got it; there would be a big mess. Identify and relish your disposition; use it to help you learn. You can start right now by determining what type of "star" you are when trying or using a new idea, object, or activity. (See Figure 1.2.) Circle the section that best describes you. Are you the same type of "star" when using computers? If you are different with computers, reflect on the reasons behind this difference.

Computer Education and Training

When to Learn

Most people agree that whether you are new to computers or highly experienced, you must have some education or training in order to use them. You can separate this process into the "when" and "what" you need to learn and "how" you can learn the needed skills and knowledge. The "when" ideally occurs before you begin using computers with children and then continues *throughout* your experiences. Often teachers receive initial training but then nothing more. We see that teachers often have more and different questions *after* they start using computers with children than before when they had limited experience. Perhaps during their earlier stages of learning, they do not know which questions to ask.

What to Learn

If you ask someone on the street what they believe are the most important skills an individual must learn about computers, you're likely to receive a variety of answers. We believe that teachers must have adequate knowledge in two primary areas; first, how to operate the computer and, second, how to use computers with young children. You must have basic computer operational skills or you will find them difficult to use with children. Your students will most likely perceive your frustration level. You must know how to turn the computer on and off, start your software programs, and do basic troubleshooting. For example, if you push the "on" switch and nothing happens, you instinctively make certain the electrical plug is securely connected in the outlet.

Using computers with young children is not the same as using computers with older students due to the different environmental settings and developmental characteristics of the children. Children learn in classrooms, child care centers, or family child care homes. Regulations and curricula vary widely across the country and even within communities. Young children learn through active engagement with their environment. They generally are emerging readers due to their age. Their teachers scaffold learning with a variety of strategies that allow individual experimentation, coaching, and large or small group experiences.

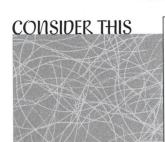

CONSIDER THIS

Teachers need ongoing training and professional experiences that increase their learning about and with computers. These professional development strategies must help teachers communicate with other professionals and implement appropriate curriculum and assessment activities with technology (NAEYC, 1996).

How to Learn

You have a variety of options for learning about computers. You could experiment by yourself, learn on-the-job, work with a friend or family member, or take a formal class through your community college or adult education program. Early childhood educators reported that they learned about computers mainly by "messing around" and from friends and family members (Bewick, 2000). Think about how you have learned other skills or gained competence in other activities. As much as possible, use those same strategies. For example, if you feel comfortable with a specific and structured plan, a formal class may be most helpful for you. However, if you prefer working at your own pace, ask someone with more advanced skills than yours to help whenever you become frustrated.

Interacting with Other Teachers.   Did you know that early childhood teachers report that, more than anything else, talking with other teachers is significantly more likely to make their computer use with children easier (Bewick, 2000)? As teachers, you need not only the time but also the opportunity to share, brainstorm, and problem-solve with others who are engaged in a similar process (Edyburn & Lartz, 1986; Landerholm, 1995). Not only will you feel less isolated, but you will also gain new strategies to support your learning. The particular strategy that works for you may depend on where you fall within a developmental sequence of teaching experience. See if any of the following information strikes a chord.

Lillian Katz (1972, 1995) proposes that teachers learn their craft in stages. Each stage has specific implications for training and staff development so that support for teachers is specific and individualized. Look at the model she suggests in Figure 1.3.

Your stage in this model indicates what type of staff development is suitable for you. Experienced teachers are more likely to learn from conferences,

Figure 1.3   Stepping through the Developmental Stages of Teaching (Katz, 1972, 1995)

Stage 4	**MATURITY**
	Teacher has perspective about self and investigates deeper and more abstract questions.
	Seminars, institutes, courses, degree programs, books, journals, conferences

Stage 3	**RENEWAL**
	Teacher asks about new developments in the field as she thinks about doing things differently than in her first three years of teaching.
	Conferences, professional associations, journals, magazines, films, visits to demonstration projects, teachers centers

Stage 2	**CONSOLIDATION**
	Teacher has decided she can survive and is ready to focus on individual children with problems.
	On-site assistance, access to specialist, colleague advice, consultants, advisors

Stage 1	**SURVIVAL**
	Generally lasts during the first year of teaching. The teacher focuses on whether she can make it through the day or week.
	Online support and technical assistance

*T*eachers share opportunities to problem solve at the computer.

articles, workshops, and seminars than those who are new to the field. Less experienced teachers respond to on-site assistance and talking with colleagues. We'll focus a bit on the less experienced teacher. We're confident that those of you with many years of successful teaching have the confidence and expertise to gain important computer skills. However, if you are someone who is concerned about how to make it through the day (Stage 1, Survival) or find yourself focused on challenging children (Stage 2, Consolidation), we recommend that you postpone using computers with your students. As some people say, your "plate is full" because basic issues with students or curriculum consume your time and energy. You could reconsider this decision after you gain more experience and your teaching skills grow. Remember, you are the primary connecting piece in the technology puzzle. You are providing connections to all the other pieces.

On the other hand, suppose that you're out of the survival stage and feeling competent about your general responsibilities in the classroom. How do you really feel about the role of computers in children's lives? Think carefully about your answer. If you believe computers are horrible and the world would be a better place without them, you need to stop reading right *now*. Unless there is a significant change in your attitude, you will have a very difficult time supporting the appropriate use of computers with young children. You most likely will offer the computer as a "busy box" option where children play games with little connection to learning. If you are not serious about the educational value of computers, your attitude conveys an unspoken message to children. They are less likely to connect their computer work with meaningful learning. As the teacher, you must model the value and use of the computer as an important tool for teaching and learning.

Another model proposed by Mark Tompkins (personal communication, September 27, 1989) suggests that adult learners begin at a stage of unconscious competence. At this point, their primary task is awareness of the scope of a project or issue. Adults progress to levels of conscious or unconscious competence in which they seek new ideas, explore old activities in new ways, and embark on a series of creative adaptations and changes. If you find yourself putting lots of time and energy into the "basics," then this may not be the right time to leap into integrating a computer learning center in your classroom.

Characteristics of Teachers Who Successfully Use Computers

So why have we spent this time talking about you? Because you are the key to completing the computer puzzle. Teachers who are interested in using computers with young children have certain things in common. Successful use of computers depends on teachers who:

- Increase their comfort level with computers
- Have knowledge and experience with computers
- Are enthusiastic about using computers with children
- Are able to view computer centers as similar to other classroom learning centers
- Can apply developmentally appropriate principles to the computer center
- Can evaluate software using principles of developmentally appropriate practice
- Can encourage young children to use computers as tools
- Recognize the goal of developing problem solvers versus programmers (Clements, 1994)
- Encourage social interaction and conversation among students who are engaged with technology
- Are willing to continue their learning about computers
- Talk with colleagues who also use computer centers and work with students of similar ages

Developing Short- and Long-Term Plans

Before you can develop a plan, you must know where to start. Throughout this chapter, we offer several issues to consider. You will know where to focus your planning efforts after you apply your learning at the chapter's conclusion. Once you determine what needs your attention, begin to think about your plan. It is critical that you must plan not only for the short term but for the longer range as well. Too often technology programs for young children fail because of poor planning for the near and distant future. When planning, consider your goal (what you want to accomplish), what resources you need, and when you need to complete it. Some people like to first think about the overall goal and then break it down into smaller steps. For example, your ultimate goal might be to have a technology center in your classroom. Currently you have no computers and need training on how to use computers with young children. Therefore, you'll focus on getting the computers as well as training. Perhaps you decide that you need eight months to achieve your goals. Divide these larger goals into smaller steps that you can accomplish in three months, one month, or even one week. Remember that for any large project, "yard by yard, it's hard; inch by inch, it's a cinch."

Collaborating with Important Stakeholders

You might have heard the term *stakeholder* before. A stakeholder is any person or group that has some vested interest in a project. If stakeholders perceive that decision makers or planners do not value their agendas and contributions, trouble is around the corner. The process in education is no different than if you are thinking about building a new highway or planning to use computers with young children. The collaborative process requires active partnerships with stakeholders. Your project's quality will increase as a result of these joint efforts with all stakeholders who have an interest in the issue.

Certainly, the director of the program is one important person. Directors influence teachers through their initiatives and determine overall quality by setting and monitoring program goals. They must consider the perspective and experience of each individual related to technology. Their knowledge of early childhood principles of development is also critical. With the race to get computers and respond to the marketing hype, they can overlook important early education principles. Directors become anxious if students are not offered the latest, greatest, best, and most high-tech experiences. If parent expectations are not being met, program enrollment can be impacted. As administrators, directors are always conscious about the bottom line.

Perhaps the technology coordinator or information system specialist is another participant in the decision regarding computers for instructional use. Is there a buyer or purchasing department? Individuals with these responsibilities must be made aware of explicit requirements for the technology, not just that it's a "best price." Remember, too, that you may have to have a "translator" between yourself and the computer guru. Sometimes technical personnel have a difficult time talking in plain English rather than precise computer terms.

Parents can be your greatest advocates. As champions of any activities that help their children succeed in school and life, their support is vital. Plan to inform and include them in your decisions about technology.

Avoiding Common Mistakes

1. *Failure to do a thorough assessment before developing your plan.*
   Sometimes in their enthusiasm, teachers or other stakeholders jump into technology without any assessment or plan. Solutions for potential issues are not addressed because no one recognizes their potential impact. Staff spirits dim as different barriers emerge. As time goes on, the grand technology project is a shadow of its former self, if it exists at all. This assessment includes teachers looking carefully at their own attitudes about and skills with computers.

2. *Avoiding or ignoring important stakeholders.*
   Some computer efforts fail because someone did not inform or consult with important stakeholders. When these groups feel disconnected, they may choose to demonstrate their concerns in unhelpful ways. Be certain to appraise anyone and everyone who has a stake in your technology effort. These groups could include parents, administrators, curriculum coordinators, advisory councils, and funding sources.

3. *Planning only for the short term (when the computers arrive) and assuming the long-term will take care of itself.*
   Avoid the initial rush of excitement and final blow of defeat by assuring that your plan contains long-term goals and strategies. Look beyond the first months of computer use into the next year and those that follow.

4. *Moving forward although you recognize that you have insufficient time, money, or support.*
   Failures with technology seem to occur most frequently when teachers move forward with their plans without resolving known issues. This is like planning a cross-country trip in your car without a road map. You'll eventually get to the other coast but the journey is likely to be difficult and involve several wrong turns. Be on the lookout for potential problems so you can try to correct them in the early stages.

Summary Points

- Planning and preparation are prerequisites for using computers effectively with young children.

- Looking at your own attitudes, values, and skills with computers is an essential step before you begin planning.

- Developing short- and long-term plans based on your self-assessment is an essential step in preparing to use computers with children.

- Collaborating with important stakeholders (parents and administrators) and other teachers who use computers increases your potential for success.

What's Next?

Now that you've examined your skills and attitudes toward computers and you are thinking about their appropriate use, you can consider how software makes a difference in your teaching. The next chapter identifies types of software, summarizes software selection criteria, discusses issues related to appropriate classroom computer use, and provides information about copyrights, licensing requirements, and other technical information.

Apply Your Learning

1. Complete the accompanying self-assessment checklist. Circle your answer to each item.

Technology Self-Assessment

1.	Yes	No	Have you ever used a computer?
	Yes	No	If yes, did you like it?
2.	Yes	No	Do you consider yourself mechanically inclined?
3.	Yes	No	Do you like to try new things?
4.	Yes	No	Are you afraid of breaking a computer?
5.	Yes	No	Are you willing to ask others for help when you face a problem?
6.	Yes	No	Do you think it is important for adults and children to know how to use computers?
7.	Yes	No	Do you think that computers can encourage creative thinking?
8.	Yes	No	Will computers benefit children's social interactions with each other?
9.	Yes	No	Is a young child capable of using a computer as a tool with minimal adult assistance?
10.	Yes	No	Do you believe that your current classroom is well equipped with a variety of materials and activities that address all domains of children's learning?
11.	Yes	No	Is there an issue, project, or priority that you must address or complete to ensure that your classroom is a high-quality environment for children?

2. Review your responses and the following descriptions. Pay particular attention to any item that was answered "No." Consider each category thoughtfully. If your mind is willing, but you identified potential challenges or obstacles during the assessment, this may not be the best time

for you to begin using computers with children. Wait until you resolve those issues to ensure greater success.

Questions 1–5 are about you as a person. If you answered "No" to any of these items, think about how critical it may be. For example, if you begin feeling stressed, will you want to pound on your computer with a hammer? Or could you stop, eat some chocolate, and return ready to solve the problem?

Questions 6–9 concentrate on philosophy and research data that support children's involvement with technology. This might be new information for you. If so, consider reading journals and other research-based literature.

The final questions, 10 and 11, look at your contextual environment. If something is missing in your current classroom or there is another pressing issue, you may need to address these areas first before beginning to use computers.

3. Based on Activity 2, what do you need to do next?

_____

_____

_____

4. If you are a teacher who is also the administrator of your program, then you have additional considerations when thinking about using computers with young children. You must adopt a broader perspective due to the range of your responsibilities. Complete the following program self-assessment to determine where you need to concentrate your efforts.

Technology Readiness Assessment Program Level

1.　　Yes　　No　　Do you feel that most of your program services to parents and children are at least adequate?

2.　　　　　Rank the following areas of program improvement for the coming year:

　　　　_____ Program improvement with administrative computers

　　　　_____ Adult literacy

　　　　_____ Classroom computer use

　　　　_____ Playground improvement

　　　　_____ Recruitment and retention of volunteers

　　　　_____ Improving parent participation

3.　　Yes　　No　　Do you have a computer(s) for administrative use?

4.　　Yes　　No　　Do you have a computer(s) for instructional use?

5.　　Yes　　No　　Did you purchase training about using your administrative software?

6.   Yes   No   Have you implemented training for your current software programs?

7.   Yes   No   Are you satisfied with your program's success in computerizing your administrative functions?

8.   Yes   No   Are you working on special initiatives in any other area of your basic program?

9.   Yes   No   Are you meeting new certification or licensing requirements and regulations?

10.   Yes   No   Is a majority of your staff new to your program?

11.   Yes   No   Are you introducing a new curriculum?

12.   Yes   No   Are you in the process of changing to or upgrading learning centers?

13.   Yes   No   Do you want to expand computer use to your classroom and/or your parent education program?

14.   Yes   No   Do you have a local computer consultant or someone on your staff who has the ability to assist with your program's effort to purchase and use computers?

15.   Yes   No   Do you have a relationship with an early childhood education department at a local community college or university?

16.   Yes   No   Does your plan include funds to support training in using classroom computers?

17.   Did you plan funds for the following requirements for setting up a computer learning center?

      Yes   No   Security of equipment

      Yes   No   Insurance

      Yes   No   Appropriate furniture

      Yes   No   Maintenance

      Yes   No   Consumable supplies (paper, printer, cartridges, diskettes, and CDs)

18.   Yes   No   Are there any major areas where basic safety and health issues need attention?

19.   Yes   No   Are you in the process of expanding your program into new areas or services?

20.   Yes   No   Have classroom staff asked about using computer activities with their young children?

21.   Yes   No   Do each of your classrooms include appropriate numbers of quality early childhood materials, furniture, and equipment?

5. How many "No" answers did you mark? Do these responses point to a particular area of concern? Write your possible solutions and plan here.

_____

_____

_____

_____

_____

_____

_____

_____

_____

_____

_____

_____

Choosing Quality Software

One way to help ensure appropriate use of technology is through your selection of software programs. Quality software is a central piece of the computer puzzle. The available software choices can be overwhelming even for the most experienced users. We shudder when outstanding early childhood educators tell us about their purchases of high-tech equivalents of drill and practice workbooks. These same teachers employ principles of active learning that engage kindergarten children in creative thinking and problem solving. For them evaluating software is different from selecting and evaluating other curriculum materials. This chapter introduces and applies principles of developmentally appropriate practice to software selection and evaluation. This contributes to better decision making by teachers.

 ## Teachers Ask

▶ *What is quality educational software for young children?*

The best software for young children provides opportunities to control a simulated environment, to explore and experiment, to create and construct, and to experience multiple solutions to challenging problems within a context they have created. It avoids drilling the same old information—colors, shape recognition, letters, or numbers.

▶ *What software do you use in educational environments such as Early Head Start for children under 3 years old?*

NAEYC and the American Academy of Pediatrics both recommend against excess screen time (TV, videos, movies, computers) and classroom computer instruction for children younger than 3. For these reasons, be cautious if anyone strongly suggests using classroom computers with infants, toddlers, or 3-year-olds. When parents or older siblings mediate the computer experience in home environments, it is a different matter. Even in this situation, experts recommend limited screen time.

▶ *How much software do I need?*

You can purchase every CD-ROM you find in the discount bin and still not have enough software. Publishers of edutainment programs consider this "throw-away" software and estimate the staying power at three months at the most. With these software programs children quickly explore the "hot spots" and figure out the "right" answers and then there is nothing else to do with the program. The best software does not present one "right" answer choice and, therefore, promotes increased engagement and exploration. Good software is like a good picture book. Children keep coming back to it. As they grow and develop, they experience the software in different ways. They have gained competence and capabilities with the technology and can use features with more self-confidence and proficiency.

▶ *What is the best source for educational software purchases?*

Although you can find many sources for edutainment software from your local electronics store to the discount bins at Wal-Mart, the best source for educational software depends on your needs. Check out software catalogs, computer magazines or journals, and the Internet. As with many purchases, the best bet is for you to shop around. If you are considering large quantities, a competitive bid process may better suit your needs.

A primary factor is whether you are purchasing quantities for an entire school or for just for one or two computers. Additionally, if you need to preview the software, the best source may be one that offers this option. In this case the software may cost a bit more.

- How to identify and categorize different types of software programs by their underlying instructional design.

- Why software is important for appropriate use of computers with young children.

- Software selection criteria that promote respect for each child's uniqueness.

- Information about copyrights, licensing requirements, and other technical information related to software purchase and use.

What Is Software Anyway?

Software is the set of coded instructions that tells the computer hardware (usually the central processing unit, CPU), what to do. Software programs are coded directions read by the hardware. These directions manipulate the text, images, sound, and voice that are produced by the computer and presented on the screen and through the speakers. You must have software in order to do anything meaningful with your computer.

Software can be installed or accessed by the computer in a variety of ways: diskette or CD-ROM drives, the hard disk, or via a modem from the Internet. Chapter 3, "Selecting Hardware," discusses these in more detail.

The Importance of Software

Without quality software, computers are useless machines that simply take up space in an already crowded classroom environment. Furthermore, because software programs create systems and goals for users, educators must use careful judgment when making selections. Therefore, selecting software for classroom instructional uses is one of the most important factors in creating an appropriate technology experience for young learners.

The formative years are critical in social, emotional, and cognitive development. Because learning during these years is acquired through multisensory experiences, children are internalizing, often at face value, what they see and hear. This is also a time when children are developing their self-identity and self-esteem.

On the positive side, software has the potential to offer children opportunities to develop sensitivities to children with disabilities or children from other cultures. Yet, in general, software publishers remain in the safe harbor of teaching basic skills rather than venturing into the riskier waters of exploring social and cultural values and lifestyles.

As it stands today, most publishers encourage children to avoid more realistic and appropriate choices by limiting children's opportunities to identify with more real-world characters. Much could be done to help children develop positive responses to cultural and racial diversity by offering software programs that enable children to explore the richness within their own and different cultures.

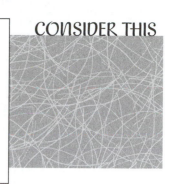

CONSIDER THIS

NAEYC (1996) believes that a professional judgment by the teacher is required to determine if a specific use of technology is age appropriate, individually appropriate, and culturally appropriate. When we value children's time and their needs for appropriate developmental learning activities, we carefully choose the software experiences we offer.

What Do We Really Want from Software?

The results are often surprising when teachers are asked to compare the criteria they use to select software with those they use to select more traditional learning materials. Frequently it appears that "cheap or inexpensive" is the top criterion for software with the implicit rationale that "if it's only $30 for a CD-ROM, what can it hurt?" When we value children's time and their needs for appropriate developmental learning activities, we choose carefully the software experiences we offer. Generally other classroom materials are chosen based on more enduring qualities such as their educational value, cultural sensitivity, ability to support and extend children's learning, curricular goals across developmental areas, and so on.

Let's carefully examine what we want computers to do in the classroom. We must reprioritize our selection criteria and stop using "cheap" as the top criterion when we purchase. Remember, the term *edutainment* developed because some software publishers veil their primarily entertainment programs as educational activities. We believe that publishers will increase this process of hiding behind the latest buzzwords and trivializing children's learning as child outcomes and program standards become more prevalent.

Software Categories

Before we look at the software selection process, take a minute to review the three categories of software generally available and determine the implications these have for educational use. There are thousands of commercially available software titles that are designated by their publishers as appropriate for young children. As you begin to grapple with the significant challenge of selecting quality software for your classroom, identifying a way to organize these media options is essential. The three following categories may help you make sense of the market of available options.

Drill and Practice

This software turns the computer into a teaching machine. The software program can be tutorial in nature. This means that when a child is presented with an activity or question there is generally only one correct response. If the child does not choose the correct response, the computer presents a series of tasks that will teach the child what the correct response should be. In this type of software the learner is passive and the computer is active.

Publishers design such drill and practice software programs to help teach specific skills, processes, or concepts. Often the activities presented to learners are primarily worksheets enhanced with music, colorful graphics, cartoons, and animation as a way to promote the entertainment or fun part of learning. Initially it may be difficult for educators to identify the "one correct answer" approach to learning because of the cute and clever animations rapidly presented by the computer. However, with careful examination the directed learning approach offered by the software becomes evident.

Simulations and Tools

Simulation and tool software allow learners to create and respond to open-ended challenges, enhancing knowledge construction (Johnson & Liu, 2000). Microworlds are child-centered, computer-simulated environments. Such software programs are similar to the tabletop manipulatives children use when they create a farm, community, or school scene using Playskool or Lego plastic and wooden animals, people, and buildings. Microworlds allow children to use the mouse to pick up objects, people, or animals and to develop role-playing scenarios on the computer screen.

In this type of software the child maintains control, acting on the computer rather than reacting to predetermined events or closed-ended problems presented by the computer. Children are permitted to experience discovery through their interactions with computers. The learner is active and the computer considered passive. Children employ their intelligence when acting on the medium rather than the software showcasing the "intelligence" of the programmer who wrote the software. Some examples include KIDWARE Neighborhoods (Farm, City, Village, and Island) and Aquarium (MOBIUS Corporation, 2002) for young learners, and Oregon Trail (MECC, 1996) and Where in the World Is Carmen Sandiego? (Broderbund, 1995) for older students.

The early years are the most critical in the development of social, emotional, and cognitive growth. Young children internalize what they see and hear through multisensory experiences. This is a time when children develop self-identity and self-esteem. Consequently, the type of images that are offered in software not only affect what children think but also what and how they feel about themselves.

Young children have many opportunities for identifying with and trying on roles. They engage in dramatic play stimulated in a variety of settings: read-aloud stories, movies and videos, and manipulatives. Software programs can also offer opportunities for children to develop and try different perspectives. They can use computer programs with favorite characters or perhaps choose characters that look like them. It is clear that software is a very powerful vehicle that has the potential to support children's early identification with positive role models.

Books on CD-ROM

Books on CD-ROM present narrative text and pictures (usually cartoons) on the computer screen. Consider these computer applications as an up-to-date version of the "listening center" medium of tape recorders and books used from the 1970s. These multimedia programs generally include options for users to select a language for the audio portion. Users go through the book from beginning to end or browse through "pages" in a nonlinear fashion of their choice. Often "hot spots" are programmed into graphics or text displays on the screen. For example, users point and click to open a mailbox and out jumps a frog as in *Grandma and Me* (Broderbund, 1995). Frequently trade books with popular cartoon characters such as Arthur or television shows such as *Blue's Clues* become software titles designed to take advantage of broad marketing efforts.

The reader of books on CD-ROM has choices for paging through the book; however, the animations, musical tunes, and availability of hot spots may interfere with the concentration of many youngsters. Children page through the book pointing and clicking to see what they can discover behind tree branches or inside mailboxes. Colorful graphics, animations, and sounds are frequently irrelevant to the story. They distract the youngster and may interfere with the learner's grasp of the materials and concepts presented in the story, including sequencing and comprehension.

How Much Software Is Enough?

With the many options available, teachers can be somewhat overwhelmed with the choices. How much software is necessary to support the teaching and learning process in the early education classroom? Here is one place where the "more is better" philosophy is not necessarily a good principle to follow. Often too many software options for children obscure the purpose and value of the computer and blur the connection between computer learning experiences and other classroom curriculum activities. This promotes confusion about the teacher's educational use of classroom computers.

Understanding what the underlying instructional design of software conveys helps teachers evaluate software. Considering the types of software available and the philosophy they reflect helps answer how much software is enough. Teachers who use individual titles tend to have many programs that may or may not integrate well with their instructional goals and the content they want children to learn. This tendency makes the computer more of a "busy-box" experience where children select from a variety of edutainment options (primarily drill and practice and CD-ROM books) with little or no tie to classroom activities outside the computer center. The "more is better" principle rules educators using this approach. However, it generally makes curriculum connections more difficult. Carefully selecting (with your educational goals in mind) and limiting the available options for children to choose enhances the possibility of meaningful and connected use of the computer even if you have lots of software.

Simulations and tool types of software are often better choices. These software programs offer the flexibility and ease of integration into a variety of learning tasks. Children use drawing, writing, and simulating to reflect their understanding of instructional concepts that are part of the curriculum experiences throughout classroom activities. You will need far fewer (in terms of the actual number) when you select these types of software programs. It is neither wise nor necessary to select a software program for every theme or project you offer. A better approach is to have several basic tool applications that provide children with easy initial use and then offer expanding complexity as children become more proficient, experienced users.

What Is the Best Source for Educational Software?

You can explore a number of sources for availability and competitive pricing now that you know the type of software you want. General retail stores, including Wal-Mart or Kmart, offer a selection of single-title edutainment and CD-ROM book software, and perhaps even a few tools or popular simulations. Electronics stores such as Best Buy or CompUSA provide a wider selection of these types of software programs, generally sold in packages designed for a single license on a single computer. School supply and software catalogs offer several software choices. Some computer magazines and journals such as *Leading and Learning with Technology* or *Computing in the Schools* also contain sources of information for educational programs.

The Internet is another resource for educational software shopping. Many software publishers have websites that describe their products and identify where or from whom they may be purchased. If you do not know the name of the publisher and you have some idea of what kind of software you need, any of the search engines can offer a plethora of choices. Google or Ask Jeeves! are often helpful in the search.

If you are interested in purchasing software in quantities, then it may be best to review your school supply catalogs or distributors that offer quantity discounts on software. Some companies have sales personnel who visit schools and demonstrate software that they carry in their catalogs. These individuals take orders and ensure that quantities are delivered. Clearly describe your needs and pricing options with your sales representative. Precisely outline how many computers will use the software and the location of these computers.

Purchase prices vary based on the type of license you are buying. For example, network versions of software titles are generally more cost-effective, but then you must have additional computing capability beyond single hard-drive, stand-alone computers. Often multiple licenses of the same title are sold in "lab" or school packs. The number of computers needing the software determines the cost. This option may suit your needs. For more tool software that can be used effectively across classrooms and grades, a school building license or site license could be the most useful. Special pricing is usually available from educational software companies and school supply catalogs.

Five Steps to Choosing Quality Software

Software decisions are important and require thought. Here's a process we recommend to enhance the possibility that you'll select quality software. Carefully following these steps results in a collection of classroom software that promotes connections between the curriculum and the computer. This process also ensures that the software you select promotes active learning that contributes to student achievement in the primary grades. First, we'll give you the steps. Next, we'll describe them in more detail.

1. Identify your educational goals.
2. Specify how you think software can assist in achieving these goals.
3. Consider curriculum content and subject areas.
4. Review the instructional strategies you use to deliver content.
5. Directly evaluate the presentation of the subject matter for accuracy and consider implicit messages related to gender, race, abilities, violence, and family structure.

Identify Your Educational Goals

Learners in the twenty-first century need to be able to (1) work collaboratively and cooperatively with others; (2) communicate clearly through oral and written modes (including graphic displays of their messages); (3) identify, describe, and define the problem that requires solving; (4) identify data sources that might offer solutions; (5) determine the authenticity of data offered from electronic and print sources; and (6) synthesize and analyze relevant information.

These goals are relevant for today's education. Many children are taught to sit down, be still, give the right answer quickly, and compete against each other—these skills were useful on the assembly line but are of little value when teams need to work together to solve complex problems. No longer can we focus on discrete skills. We need to teach in a way so as *not* to impart knowledge but instead to help children construct their own interpretations, filling in the gaps, and interpreting in order to understand.

Specify How You Think Software Can Assist in Achieving These Goals

How can software assist us in achieving our educational goals? What do we expect of classroom computers? How can our educational goals be facilitated by activities that are technology based and congruent with how young children learn? We need to determine what we expect of computers. Do we just get computers because everyone else has? What types of software programs match our educational goals for young children? Computers at the very least should provide opportunities that promote and enhance children's construction of knowledge, facilitate positive social interactions, offer exposure to diversity in contexts that do not promote stereotyping, allow children to explore representational settings, and provide environments for creating make-believe play.

Consider Curriculum Content and Subject Areas

Young children have many opportunities for identifying with and trying on roles in dramatic play settings, read-aloud stories, and movies. Software programs also offer opportunities for children to develop and take on the perspectives of favorite characters within this medium. It is clear that software is a very powerful vehicle that supports children's early identification with characters. One reason software seems to be so powerful is its interactivity. This means the child actively engages with the software and controls what happens on the screen. The negative side of this power is that there are often stereotypes that are portrayed in children's software. In addition, there exists a serious imbalance in the gender of characters

*S*upport girls' use of computers by selecting software that includes female characters.

offered by most software publishers. A recent review of software for young children indicates that there are three times more male characters than female characters (Buckleitner, 2000). This imbalance can seriously affect young girls' interest and interaction with technology.

Ironically, today's software tries to avoid issues of gender and race by presenting cartoon or animal characters instead of more realistic representations of characters. Even with these attempts to be neutral and non-controversial, stereotypes still persist. For example, examine how "female" animal characters are portrayed compared to "male" animal characters. Often females are supportive and docile, whereas males are aggressive and risk takers. Or the software promotes more male-associated characteristics, such as shooting or destroying objects on the screen.

Software programs frequently offer children the opportunity to get rid of mistakes by "blowing up" their creations instead of simply erasing or starting over. As a metaphor for solving problems or getting rid of mistakes, "blowing up" is problematic. In the context of a computer software experience, it is more problematic than in the context of television or video. Children are empowered to control the computer software and instead of being passive viewers of what appears on the screen, with the computer they become active decision makers about what takes place on the screen.

CONSIDER THIS

The power of technology to influence children's learning and development requires that attention be paid to eliminating stereotyping of any group and eliminating exposure to violence, especially as a problem-solving strategy (NAEYC, 1996). When we examine the many examples of violence as a response to problem solving within software programs that permit a child to thoughtlessly press a key to blow up or "waste" someone or something, it should cause us to consider the implications of such empowerment. Software programs that empower children to freely blow up or destroy without thought of the actual consequences of their actions can only zfurther the disconnection between personal responsibility and violent outcomes.

Review Your Curriculum and Instructional Strategies

This is an essential requirement in the software selection process. Its answer depends on your understanding of how young children learn (the pedagogy), your approach to providing learning opportunities for young children (the curriculum), and your instructional design choice (constructivist or instructivist).

Let's review the learning process young children use. We must consider what we know about how young children learn—pedagogy, if you will. This

*T*eachers ensure that computer experiences are meaningful for young children by choosing quality software.

includes examining the strategies children use for exploration and learning. Children learn through play—moving from the active, physical exploration of the environment to more abstract thinking. Children learn best through active, hands-on teaching methods such as games (simulations) and dramatic play. Children learn to reason and communicate by engaging in meaningful conversation with teachers (many teachers talk at children, not with them; telling is not teaching). Children learn from child-initiated, self-directed activities. Children construct knowledge from direct experiences that are meaningful and challenging. Schools (and parents) that demand too much too soon are setting kids off on the road to failure. For these reasons and others we concur with NAEYC that classroom computer use with children younger than age 3 is not appropriate. The American Academy of Pediatrics goes further and suggests strict limits on the amount of time this age group is exposed to screen technology in general, including television, videos, and computers.

Many educators wonder about using computers in child care centers and Early Head Start programs that enroll children younger than 3 years old. Some have experiences using computers with their own young children, citing examples of their child climbing up on their lap, watching the screen, and playing on the keyboard. Children seem to enjoy the computer experience in this way. Using the computer at home in this manner is simply different than use in a classroom setting where there are many more children and fewer adults. Children younger than 3 years old in classroom settings are working on many other skills and concepts and simply do not need the additional challenges of computer use to complicate the social interactions and environment.

Keeping in mind how young children learn and the different instructional strategies you use to organize and deliver curriculum will assist you as you evaluate appropriate classroom software. Let's examine what kind of instructional strategies engage students in an active learning process.

Requirements for Authentic Learning. Newmann and Wehlage (1993) have identified five requirements of authentic instruction. The first is reflected in the type of thinking required of students. Engaged learners are required to manipulate information in ways that transform their meaning and implications, such as when students combine facts and ideas in order to synthesize, generalize, explain, hypothesize, or arrive at some conclusion or interpretation. Manipulating information and ideas through these processes allows students to solve problems and discover new meanings and understandings.

Depth of knowledge is a second requirement. Deep knowledge is produced, in part, by covering fewer topics in systematic and connected ways. For children, knowledge is deep when it concerns central ideas of a topic of discipline and when they can make clear distinctions, develop arguments, solve problems, construct explanations, and work with relatively complex understandings.

Connectedness to the world beyond the classroom is a third essential requirement of authentic instruction. The class has value and meaning beyond the instructional context. A lesson gains in authenticity the more there is a connection to the larger social context within which students live. This can happen when students address real-world public problems or when students use personal experiences as a context for applying knowledge.

Substantive conversation reflecting the requirement of interaction and communication necessary to understand the nature of a subject sharing of ideas is evident and children serve in various roles within this evolving communication process (e.g., peer tutors, mentors, colleagues, etc.). Dialogue promotes improved collective understanding of the theme or topic.

The final requirement (identified by Newmann and Wehlage) is social support for student achievement. This means that there are high expectations, mutual respect among students, and inclusion of all students in the learning process.

CONSIDER THIS

Early childhood educators should promote equitable access to technology for all children and their families. Children with special needs should have increased access when this is helpful (NAEYC, 1996). This means that there are high expectations, mutual respect among students, and software programs that support inclusion.

Directly Evaluate the Presentation of the Subject Matter for Accuracy and Implied Messages

The type of images projected in on-screen technologies affect not only what children think but also what and how they feel about themselves. Prejudice, bias, and the power of violence are passed, often insidiously, through the books, materials, and the media (movies, videos, television, and software) to which children are exposed. A good example of this phenomenon is the *Mighty Morphin' Power Rangers,* whose characters perpetuate both stereotypes and violence. If this is currently one of the most popular television programs children watch and is now available as a software product, what responsibility are we taking for young children regarding exposure to violence and negative stereotypes? We must seriously consider this question. Research clearly documents the impact passive viewing of violence on television has on young children in terms of their desire to model and act out what they see. How then are we to infer that children's active involvement with software that promotes control of violence on the screen impacts their behavior?

We condemn the seemingly endless and purposeless violence that regularly erupts in our urban and suburban schools nationwide. The youngsters responsible for these violent acts are all a part of our "passive television viewing audience." These youngsters have been exposed over their lifetimes to unlimited exemplars of violence (on television and in movies) as an acceptable problem-solving strategy. How will this new generation of computer users, who are no longer merely passive viewers of the action on the screen but are now "empowered" to control the action, respond to problems they face when they grow up?

CONSIDER THIS

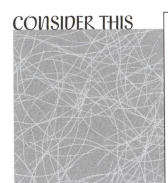

The power of technology to influence children's learning and development requires that attention be paid to eliminating stereotyping of any group and eliminating exposure to violence, especially as a problem-solving strategy (NAEYC, 1996). Consequently, the type of images that are projected in on-screen technologies affect not only what children think but also how they feel about themselves.

Technical Details

You might wonder what kind of technical information you need to know to be sure the software works on your hardware. Determining what software matches your computer specifications can be one of the most daunting challenges. There are a few very specific and technical terms that are often mentioned when you are trying to determine whether software you select works on your computer. Understanding these terms at a basic level should help you in determining whether the software requirements match your hardware configuration. Here's a summary of key terms to assist you in the process.

Drives are usually CD-ROM although a 3 ½-inch-high density drive is generally included. Software CDs are the most frequent medium for distribution of software programs. The software program can be installed on the hard disk or run from the CD located in the drive. The speed of the CD-ROM drive will impact the responsiveness of the software program especially when there are a lot of graphics, animation, and speech files required for use. Internet delivery of software directly to your modem-equipped central processing unit (CPU) is another option that is gaining popularity.

Another option for the CD-ROM drive that usually is "read only" (meaning that it can only install or play software programs and that it cannot be used to save data or information you are creating) is the read/write CD-ROM drive. This type of drive permits you to use writeable CDs and then, when you "write" to the CD, you put your own information on it.

Hardware configuration and system requirements refer to the type of computer you plan to use with the software you are purchasing.

Operating system is most commonly Windows (various versions include 98, 2000, XP, and NT) or Mac/Apple (version 9).

Printers must be purchased that ensure compatibility with your computer. That is, they must include software (referred to as *printer drivers*) that is compatible with your operating system. A Windows printer may not print in a DOS environment and vice versa.

*P*rinters *are an* essential *component of early literacy experiences.*

RAM means "random access memory" and refers to how much memory is required for the software program to run.

Available storage space or read-only memory (ROM) refers to available space on the hard disk, generally specified in megabytes or gigabytes required.

Speed of processor designates how quickly your computer can load the software (access the ROM storage) and process auditory, graphic, and text files so they are responsive to user input. For example, Pentium refers to the speed of an internal processor.

Sound cards or chips, which record with a built-in or plugged-in microphone, permit you to put your voice files into the computer. Playback functions for these chips are absolutely essential for young emergent readers.

This summary of hardware specifications and system requirements should get you started. You are ready to tackle the specs of hardware requirements, short of becoming a computer scientist. Now on to additional considerations related to software selection. Let's examine the issue of technical support.

Technical Support

Often a software publisher provides customer service to assist with technical problems that might arise during installation and use of its software. Toll-free technical support is an important asset, especially for new users. Carefully consider your own individual requirements for support and the nature of the support available from your software source or the software publisher of the product you purchase.

Be sure to note whether technical support or customer support is toll free with no charge for troubleshooting your installation or actually talking with a technical representative. Confirm that the 1-800 phone number advertised is for free technical support and not just for ordering software products! Sometimes publishers maintain toll-free lines exclusively for sales and ordering information and use a different system for support. It never hurts to inquire before you purchase. At least there will be no surprises if you have clarified the company's policy ahead of time.

Occasionally there is actually a charge for telephone support beyond the cost of the long-distance call. Be sure to check the nature of the support offered by the software publisher you select. More and more frequently the Internet website of a software publisher offers technical support for users.

The software publisher may require you to register to be eligible to access the toll-free support. You simply complete the registration form included with the software packaging and either mail or electronically send it to the publisher. Sometimes you can also receive updated information and helpful hints.

Copyrights and Licensing Issues

When you purchase a software program, you are actually buying the privilege to use it according to the license agreement. It is not your right to give the software away to other people if you keep a copy of it for yourself. Specific and legally binding copyright information in the form of a software license accompanies all software programs. The information generally specifies the type of software license purchased. Some common designations include single hard drive, multiuser, and a network or site license version. This document also includes installation and warranty provisions.

The U.S. copyright laws and international treaty provisions protect software that is developed in the United States. Therefore, you must treat software and accompanying copyrighted material (manuals, instructions, and guides) like any other copyrighted material. You may not remove or copy any trademarks or copyrights attached or associated with the software and supporting materials. This means generally that it is illegal to make copies of software for your friends and family.

Your software license specifies exactly how many computers are authorized to have the software you have purchased installed or used. There is a distinct difference (both in terms of cost and capability) between a single hard disk version of the software and a network version of the software. Generally a single hard disk version is more costly and only is used on one computer. Additional licenses and CD-ROMs can be purchased for use on additional computers.

In the single hard disk installation the work and files of the user remain on that particular computer. This is entirely different in a network situation. The software is installed on a file server that runs a number of connected workstations. These workstations permit a student to use any of the connected workstations to access the software and his or her individual work. All of an individual's work can be collected and organized no matter which workstation was used in its creation. In addition the pricing for the network version of a software program is more economical because it is installed on one file server and distributed to many different workstations.

Summary Points

- Criteria for selecting software should reflect the criteria you use for choosing other educational media and materials that support your curriculum goals.
- Classroom computer use is most developmentally appropriate for children 3 years old and older.

- The number of software programs you need is directly tied to your educational goals and the instructional design of the software that links your curriculum with the computer center.
- Copyrights and licensing requirements affect software use in the classroom and early childhood educators must be aware of these.

What's Next?

Now that you understand the importance of selecting software that is appropriate for your classroom, you will want to become knowledgeable about the process of selecting hardware that supports the software you choose. The next chapter provides a comprehensive discussion of the process. It introduces language and terminology that are necessary for you to communicate effectively with hardware vendors when you discuss your technology needs.

Apply Your Learning

1. *Selecting software for your target audience*
   Complete the following chart as part of determining your audience for software use.

SOFTWARE AUDIENCE

Who	Languages	Disabilities or Other Special Considerations
Children Ages 3–4		
Children Ages 5–8		
Parents		
Teaching Staff		
Administrative Staff		
Others		

2. In this chapter several categories of software were identified. Inventory the software available for students in the primary grades in your classroom or your school library. Review each software program and determine which of the three categories discussed in this chapter is most like the software you are reviewing. After you have identified at least one software program that corresponds to each of the three categories, complete the evaluation form in Activity 3 for each software program.

SOFTWARE CATEGORIZATION

Software Title	Drill and Practice	Simulations	Books on CD-ROM

3. *Software Evaluation, Part 1*

Go to a software store where you can try various software programs at a workstation. Select software programs that you might consider purchasing. Complete the following evaluation form as you review new software.

SOFTWARE EVALUATION FORM

Title:	Teacher:		
1. **Software Type** (circle one)	Drill and Practice	Simulation	Books on CD-ROM

2. **Educational Content**	**Your Comments**
a. Is the information accurate?	
b. Is it appropriate for young children?	
c. Does it enhance the content of your program?	
d. Is it relevant to a new theme you would like to develop?	
e. Does the software reflect the backgrounds of all children, families, and staff in the program?	
f. Are the artistic representations of different ethnic groups, males and females, and differently abled people appropriate? If not, how do you recommend these graphic presentations be enhanced or changed?	
g. Does the program reflect ethnic groups in the community, state, and U.S. society in their families, at work, and at play?	
h. Are women and men of different ethnic backgrounds doing jobs in the home?	
i. Are women and men of various ethnic backgrounds doing jobs outside the home that include a variety of work (e.g., blue-collar work, white-collar, artistic work)?	
j. Are elderly men and women of various ethnic backgrounds doing a variety of activities?	
k. Are differently abled people of various ethnic backgrounds working, spending time with their families, and playing?	
l. Are different family lifestyles represented, including single moms, two dads, two moms, a mom and grandmother, interracial and multiethnic families, foster families, families with differently abled members, and low-income and middle-class families? What changes would you suggest to make this software program more effective and sensitive to issues of diversity?	

3. **Developmental Appropriateness**
   Does this software offer your children:

   a. A chance to create something unique?

   b. Opportunities to problem solve?

   c. Experiences that enhance self-esteem?

   d. An introduction to new skills and concepts?

   e. Social interaction?

Your Comments

4. **Using Software:**   Order these items from 1 = most appropriate to 4 = least appropriate.

   _____ When operated by an individual child

   _____ When several children took turns on the same computer

   _____ When two children worked side by side

   _____ When an adult worked with a group of children

5. **Operation of the Software Program**

   a. Which input devices can children use successfully? Circle all that apply.

   Mouse   Joystick   Keyboard   Touch window

   b. If available, do children understand the picture menus? How could they be improved?

   c. Do children easily learn the necessary procedures to operate the software?

6. **Evaluation**

   After considering each of these items, would you use this software program with your children? Why or why not?

4. *Software Evaluation, Part 2*
   Now that you have had considerable experience in evaluating software using this form, consider revising the form so that it better meets your needs. Have one of your colleagues use your newly created form to evaluate a piece of software.

5. Identify the person(s) in your organization responsible for purchasing classroom software. Find out the about the selection and review process. What percentage of the software currently available for your school or center meets the criteria for quality software? Do you think the current process ensures that quality software is available for your classroom? How could the process be improved?

6. Complete a cost comparison of at least three software programs you selected from different vendors.

SOFTWARE COST COMPARISON

Software Title	Source	Cost	Shipping and Handling	Tax	Total Cost
1.					
2.					
3.					
4.					

Remember, if you order from a catalog rather than directly from the software publisher, ask about procedures and policies for installation and technical support.

Selecting Hardware

In Chapter 2 you learned about the different kinds of software available. Now that you know what kind of software you want to use in your classroom, you need to consider the hardware requirements. Where do you begin? How much technical knowledge is necessary? Are you going to consider donated equipment? How can you factor hardware obsolescence into your planned purchase? This chapter is designed to help you answer these questions.

Teachers Ask

▶ *How many computers should you have in a classroom?*

For prekindergarten classrooms with twenty or fewer children, two computers with a shared printer make a learning center arrangement that generally suits classroom needs. As children move through the elementary grades and become more proficient in using the computer for word processing and other tool applications, the computer takes on a greater role in supporting academic work. In this case the number of computers should increase to about one computer for every five children. Remember Seymour Papert's apt observation that one computer for a class of thirty children is like thirty children sharing a pencil (1980). If you are truly integrating the computer, and the teacher and children use technology as a tool, then having one computer for every five children is essential. The number required is much fewer if the computer is only a "busy box" or "babysitter" for children who are done with their work.

▶ *What do I need? What will it cost, and how long will it last?*

We recommend that a basic classroom computer system include the computer unit with monitor, CD and diskette drives, input devices, and printer. The cost of these items continually decreases. This means you can buy more computing power for the money you spend. Although you probably do not need this capacity, it extends the useful life of your computer. Consider your classroom needs and comparison shop for the best deal. Remember that most computer salespeople are not educators and do not have much experience in using computers to support teaching and learning. A valued colleague with experience in this area is often the best source of guidance to ensure your computer setup truly meets your needs.

Generally, a computer setup with printer will last about three years. By then the advances in operating features and software capabilities to use these features will render today's newest computer inadequate.

Two computers (with a shared printer) provide sufficient technology for a prekindergarten class with twenty children.

◗ How can I use free or donated computers?

As businesses and government agencies purchase new technology, there is an abundance of old computers that are no longer needed. It is possible to effectively use these computers for classroom purposes; however, they may need to be repaired and upgraded to run current software. Maintenance costs to keep them running may be higher. Consider carefully the ramifications of this "free" hardware. Everything comes with a price. Free hardware and service costs might equal the cost of a newer system.

◗ Mac or Windows—does it matter?

More and more software being published is "hybrid." This means that the software runs on computers with either a Mac or Windows operating system. Although Apple/Mac had an initial surge of popularity in the school/education market, things have changed considerably. Price has become a dominant factor in selecting computers for schools, and the competitive prices of Windows computers have eroded Apple/Mac's early lead. There are more manufacturers and component part suppliers that produce Windows computers and only one company that manufactures Apple/Macs.

After Reading This Chapter, You'll Know

- Minimum hardware requirements and services necessary to ensure success.
- How to identify hardware sources and comparison shop.
- Basic troubleshooting techniques for your computer system.
- How to ensure furniture supports your system configuration for ease of use and accessibility.

Purchasing Hardware

Selecting appropriate hardware for your classroom computer center has never been easier. Today's computers, even the least expensive, off-the-shelf models, come with all the bells and whistles you'll need to run quality educational software for your students and tool applications for yourself.

Planning for Technology

As many more early childhood educators realize that computers are not just another educational fad but that appropriate experiences can benefit young children's learning, they become motivated to acquire technology. However, cost factors and in many cases a lack of knowledge and experience with technology affect our decision to move forward. We want to ensure that our resources for hardware are well spent and our computers meet our needs. This requires deliberate planning. Initial costs of hardware and software, maintenance, expendable supplies, and in-service training are all factors that go into the equation. Creating successful classroom computer experiences depend on adequate planning for technology purchase and implementation.

CONSIDER THIS

As early childhood educators become active participants in a technological world, they need in-depth training and ongoing support to be adequately prepared to make decisions about technology and to support its effective use in learning environments for children (NAEYC, 1996). We want to ensure that our resources for hardware are well spent and our computers meet our needs. Careful preparation reduces the likelihood of expensive mistakes.

The following steps summarize a process for acquisition of classroom hardware. Each of the five steps includes specific questions you should address as part of the planning process. For example, a key question under the first step "what is the purpose of the classroom computer system?" may initially appear to have a rather straightforward, obvious answer. However, consider that in addition to using the computer for instructional purposes with young children, you might also want to offer teachers support for any of the following:

- Online in-service training and professional development.
- Internet access for information gathering and instructional purposes.
- Administrative tasks or record-keeping functions such as attendance and lesson planning or communication with colleagues and parents via e-mail.

With these options in mind, the answer to the question of the purpose of the classroom computer system becomes more broad-based and comprehensive. Your response to this question defines the scope of your plans for computer use. Comprehensive and thoughtful solutions emerge as you and your colleagues pursue the planning process.

Steps in Purchasing a Computer System

Step 1: Assess your needs.
- What is the purpose of the classroom computer system?
- What software applications will be used?
- Will the system be used without connection to another computer (stand-alone) or in a network with other units?
- What minimum requirements do the software programs have?
- Will a printer or other peripherals be necessary?
- Is connecting to the Internet desirable?
- What is the available budget?
- What technical support is available and what does it cost?

- What kinds of warranty and service plans are available?
- How might this system meet expanding requirements as innovations in software and hardware emerge?

Step 2: Update yourself on what's available in the hardware market.
- Read computer magazines, vendor ads, sales literature, newspaper ads, and so on.
- Review computer company websites on the Internet.
- Review articles in magazines such as *PC Week* that evaluate hardware and printers.
- Consult trusted vendors and colleagues.

Step 3: Once you have completed steps 1 and 2, you are ready to:
- List the minimum specifications you desire.
- Specify additional information you want including warranties and technical support availability.
- Provide list of specifications to local hardware vendors and investigate the cost of this specific hardware setup from Internet mail-order sites that specialize in hardware configurations.
- Specify the time frame and deadlines for purchase and installation.
- When possible, ask for demonstrations.

Step 4: Compare cost estimates from available price quotes.
- Be sure all specifications are met.
- Compare any additional services that go beyond what you have requested. "Added value" frequently means these services or products are offered at no additional charge. Be certain they are items you actually want or can use.
- Accept the price quote that is most advantageous.

Step 5: On receipt of the hardware system:
- Check the components to be sure that everything is in working order and there is no apparent damage.
- Complete and return all registration cards (or register online or via fax). Be sure to make and keep copies of the registration cards if you use the mail-in option.
- Document serial numbers, warranty information, purchase date, technical support numbers, and so on.
- Keep all documentation, diskettes, CD-ROMs, and reference materials provided with your new systems.

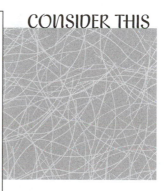

CONSIDER THIS

Early childhood educators should provide a learning environment that recognizes children have individual preferences, patterns of development, ability levels, strengths, learning styles, and language backgrounds (Head Start/Title I Performance Standards, DHHS, 1998). Appropriate computer hardware can reflect the uniqueness of each child and family when teachers keep this principle in mind.

Computer System Components

We must identify two distinct operating systems that exist before we begin a piece-by-piece analysis of what actually goes into a computer system. The operating system used by the computer predetermines many of the features and options available. Generally computers can be divided into two platforms—Macs and PCs. The information we are providing primarily refers to Windows desktop personal computers. Although the Mac is a fine alternative, only one company, Apple, sells it. There are only a few models available and not as many options exist. That makes purchasing a Mac much simpler. Major PC hardware manufacturers produce a full line of computer systems using the Windows operating system. PCs have operating systems that are referred to as "open architecture" and that means that many computer manufacturers use the same or similar operating systems. This enables hardware manufacturers to produce component parts that can be configured into a system with the Windows operating system on a piecemeal basis. Macintosh computers, on the other hand, come with a unique and special (proprietary) operating system that cannot be integrated easily with PC components.

Central Processor

The central processing unit (CPU) is the hardware that is the "guts" of your system. The internal parts of the CPU can include the modem, motherboard, fan, electric components, cards, and CD-ROM and disk drive

units. These same internal parts are contained in a "box" (usually rectangular or square). These internal parts can be arranged in the box so they are horizontal (desktop) or vertical (called a tower). Your space availability and furniture for the computer center can help you decide which option (desktop or tower) is better for your classroom learning center setup. The system unit is configured with a processor that accesses and displays the graphics, sound, and other features of the software you are using. The speed of the processor relates to how fast your system handles the requirements of the software. Processors come in a variety of speeds—here the faster, the better. The term *megahertz* (MHz) denotes speed.

Memory

Random access memory (RAM) refers to the availability of memory used during processing tasks. RAM availability is denoted by the term *megabytes*

(MB). Systems that run Windows 98 or higher require 32 MB or more to function efficiently.

Another type of memory, ROM, refers to the storage capacity of the system. In other words, how many and what size sound, graphic, and text files can your system store when these files are not in immediate use in RAM? ROM size is designated in megabytes or gigabytes. System storage is usually maintained on the hard drive of the unit. The storage space on the hard drive is considered "cheap" and the bigger the size of the hard drive the better. When you hear the size of storage capability generally available, you think you'll never use all that space; however, consider that the Windows operating system can take up to 100 MB of space depending on what components are installed.

Multimedia Components

Disk Drives.   Usually a 3.5-inch diskette drive is a standard feature on most system units. This permits you to save, transfer, and load files from other sources. The capacity of the 3.5-inch diskette is lower than a CD-ROM drive.

A CD-ROM (compact disc) drive is necessary to load and play many multimedia and music CDs. A CD-ROM only reads files. High speed is crucial to maintain children's interest and interactive engagement when you use the CD to access and use edutainment multimedia software that is not installed on your hard drive.

CD-ROM drives can also be used for writing data, graphics, and sound files from your system unit or the Internet. A CD-ROM drive that is also a CD-Writer has the capacity to write data to a recordable CD. Look for the "R" (recordable) in the specifications in the manual or on the box. The speed of reading and writing (designated by a number and an X) can be an important consideration when determining your needs. These features enable you to easily transport files from one system to another. For example, if you download music files, photographs, or videos from the Internet, writing these very large files to recordable CDs for storage is very efficient and convenient.

Music and Speech.   The sound card enables the computer to play MIDI files (music made from instrument samples) and wave files (digitized human voice and other real sounds). The chip that enables the MIDI or wave files to be accessed can be installed in the system "box" on a sound card or actually "on board." An "on board" sound chip is an integrated part of the motherboard.

The sound is amplified through external speakers or speakers that are an integrated part of the system unit. Internal speakers may be more desirable because they take up less space and there are fewer wires; however, they offer less flexibility in terms of amplification of sound and quality of playback of the sound/speech files.

A microphone can be available as part of the system or as an extra plug-in device. This device supports recordable speech and sometimes can be used to customize the software with your own voice files. The built-in microphone lacks the flexibility of being able to be located close to the source of the sound. An external handheld microphone can be more easily moved to the source of the sound. This option facilitates ease of use by teachers and young children.

CONSIDER THIS

Early childhood educators should promote equitable access to technology for all children and their families. Children with special needs should have increased access when this is helpful (NAEYC, 1996). For users with special needs other types of input devices are available. We recommend that the selection of a special input device or adaptive software be made in consultation with a technology-experienced special educator.

Input Devices

Generally the mouse or keyboard offers accessibility to the computer. Other types of input devices are available for users with special needs. For example, an adaptive peripheral, such as a switch, promotes accessibility for a child with certain physical disabilities or motor impairments. We recommend that the selection of a special input device or adaptive software for special needs children be made in consultation with a technology-experienced special educator. This decision should be individualized, based on the child's specific functional abilities and the computer setup being used.

Keyboards.   Most keyboards come in the standard QWERTY configuration. This means that the keys are assembled beginning on the left, above the "home" row with the letters Q, W, E, R, T, and Y. Another option, marketed heavily to early childhood educators, begins the layout with the

letter A in the place of the Q and goes through letters in alphabetical order. The arrangement of keys is designed to help youngsters who are beginning to use the keyboard in word processing. Generally, children must "say" the alphabet in order to find the letters. This layout may be helpful initially; however, as children become more experienced with literacy, word processing, and computers, these early training experiences could inhibit their abilities to learn touch-typing. Also, we want children to generalize their skills of word processing to computers equipped with the more widely used QWERTY keyboard.

We do not recommend teaching touch-typing to children until about second or third grade. Children younger than about 7 years old have small hands and cannot manage the finger span or dexterity for this skill. At this young age, we just want children to experience inputting letters in the most comfortable and efficient way they can manage. This is most likely not placing fingers on the home row and then trying to reach letters above and below while maintaining this position. Many young children have not yet established letter recognition and familiarity with letter names.

For the very youngest and inexperienced users (3-year-olds who do not have older or experienced children as role models for appropriate keyboard use) we recommend that you, the teacher, sign on to the computer and the children's software. Then store the keyboard out of sight, perhaps behind the monitor. Storing the keyboard this way eliminates some of the temptation inexperienced users exhibit to bang on the keyboard. This keyboard banging usually happens when children have not established an understanding of cause and effect that their input has on computer use. Once the teacher has used the keyboard to take story dictation from children and children have "made books" as a result of these literacy activities, the keyboard becomes much more meaningful to young children. It can then be returned to its place at the computer station and support children's modeling of the teacher's taking story dictation.

There are three prerequisites to children's independent use of the keyboard: (1) understanding cause and effect, (2) gaining more experience with the computer, and (3) teachers demonstrating the use of the keyboard for story dictation. Then children are ready to be gradually introduced to use of the keyboard.

One key that is problematic for educators of young children is the key that with one stroke moves the software application to the task bar and returns the user to the operating system or desktop screen. The key generally has a Windows icon. This is very inconvenient for children and for teachers, too, when children exit accidentally from the software they are using through a single key press. Getting back into the children's software requires adult help. There are  software solutions that can prevent this accidental exiting. Inquire of your vendor about software solutions or pay the few extra dollars to have a special keyboard that does not include this key.

Mouse Units. The mouse is a popular input device and most multimedia software programs require mouse input. There are two ways to plug the mouse unit into the back of the computer. One is through the pointer port and the other is through the serial port. An alternative is a mouse that does not require a physical attachment to the computer. This may be handy because it increases flexibility; however, a  mouse that's not attached may wander to other parts of the classroom or building. In any case, establish a "mouse house" where children put the mouse when they are finished with their computer use. This can be as simple as designating the mouse pad as the mouse's house.

Mouse units usually come with a right and left button. Some software requires specific use of one or the other of these buttons to access different functions. A third button is available to provide instant access to the Internet. Do *not* purchase this type of mouse unit for your classroom use. This instant access may be very convenient for adults who easily use the third button intentionally. However, for youngsters with evolving mouse motor coordination it is a definite *no*!

Other Input Devices

The variety of input devices available is enormous and growing. Some of these options are targeted strictly for very young users. For example, there is an input device that is a large plastic steering wheel and, depending on the direction it turns, the cursor moves through a fantasy of color, sound, and animated video sequences. Gimmicky input devices, joysticks, specially arranged keyboard layouts or large colorful keys, and other types of input devices, including even touch windows, are primarily a boon to marketers of these products. The majority of young children (excluding those with specific disabilities) do not require special input devices. At most, young children are better served with a child-sized version of the real thing. For example, some early childhood educators have found that a smaller than standard size mouse makes mouse input easy and efficient for young children.

Although a slightly smaller than standard mouse makes sense for small hands, a keyboard that is tiny raises some issues. Tiny keyboards are designed with the size of children's small hands (finger span) and dexterity in mind. Most young children are not ready to touch type and the very small size of the keys combined with the evolving fine motor coordination of young children make it difficult for children to find and accurately press the keys they want to use. Such tiny keyboards also make it difficult for adults to efficiently use the keyboard for story dictation or their own tasks.

The following scenario illustrates dramatically how we must consider carefully the alternative input options being touted by marketers and how children quickly move to model the computer-using behavior of their teachers and parents. We have encountered one hardware vendor who actively promoted built-in touch screens when selling to Head Start and other centers enrolling 3- and 4-year-olds. The vendor's pitch was that touch windows were absolutely essential for children's easy use of the computer, rendering the entire system worthless in their absence. Interestingly, this option added significantly to the high cost of the computer setup.

For administrators and educators (especially those who are not mouse proficient and a bit intimidated by technology) the touch screen seems so easy to use. However, once the computer was introduced to children and they saw the teaching staff using the mouse, they, too, wanted to use the mouse. No amount of encouragement would convince the children to use the touch screen instead. The extra money spent to equip the computer with a touch screen could have been much better spent on quality software instead of the edutainment package bundled with the hardware.

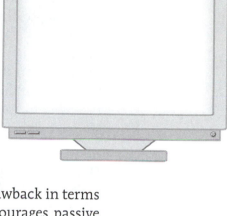

Monitor or Video Display.   The monitor or display is the TV-like unit that enables us to see and respond to what the software does when it is accessed through the CPU. Monitors are available in different screen sizes. These measurements refer to the diagonal length and are from 14 to 21 inches. The larger the unit is, the more "TV-like" the image is for young children. This may be a drawback in terms of children's interpretation of the media as one that encourages passive viewing as opposed to interactive use. Space considerations also become more of a concern with larger monitors.

Video RAM is a feature that is stated in terms of megabytes. Usually 1 MB is sufficient for most frequently used classroom applications. This RAM can reside as a chip on the motherboard or on a separate video card. Video RAM determines the maximum amount of color, depth, and resolution that can be displayed.

Printer

A printer is an absolutely essential peripheral for any computer setup. The prediction of the "paperless" office has never really materialized. Some contend that computers have generated even more paper. Most users seem to find it important to review a hard copy of their documents any time even minor edits change format or text!

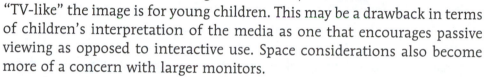

The availability of printouts is absolutely essential for young children. For these users many of the early, appropriate experiences at the computer incorporate letters, words, and literacy. Printouts support opportunities for children to view the product of their interactive computer activities.

Now that the need for a printer is established, the question of which printer to purchase becomes central. There are several considerations:

1. Color versus black and white
2. Quality of output (described in dots per inch)
3. Speed of the printing process
4. Durability of the printer

Color versus Black Ink.   The choice of color printer relates directly to expendable supplies—how much is the replacement cartridge and how long does a cartridge last? The actual cost of the color printer is no longer as much an issue as is the cost of the replacement cartridges. You'll need to determine these charges for the printer you are considering.

Many classrooms have black ink printers. Then the children take their printouts to the art center to customize them with color, using crayons, markers, or paints. Here is a typical scenario: A child's printout is complete; her turn at the computer is finished. She takes her paper and writes her name on it or adds color details. This strategy frees up the computer for other children's use. It also helps children understand that they can still use other media (pencils, crayons, and markers) to write—the word processor isn't the only way to write!

Quality of Output.   The quality of the printer output is primarily an issue for those who want to use printers for more than children's work. Camera-ready artwork cannot be produced from most low-end color or black ink printers. Moderate quality is acceptable for most classroom needs. You may sacrifice some quality when your printer uses less ink, prints more slowly, or is a less expensive model.

Speed of Printing.   How quickly a color printout is produced depends on the software being used and the printer. Once children select the print option, they are anxious to get the printouts. Quick printing is an important consideration. We found that if the printer is set up so children can watch the printing process, they are much more patient than if the printer is out of sight. We recommend that the printer be set up in a way to facilitate their independent use of both the printer and retrieving their printouts.

Durability.   Durability and ease of use are important not only because of the amount of printing required in literacy-rich learning environments but also because we are helping young learners become independent in the process. Children enjoy making their own stories and books at the computer center. They can learn to be gentle in retrieving their printouts. Nevertheless, the printer you select should take into consideration these young users and their emerging needs for supported independence.

We have one word of caution about accepting donations of used hardware from private sources, businesses, or government agencies. Do not accept computers with operating systems that are incompatible with or limit the software choices you have available. On the surface this generous donation of used hardware appears to be just what you need. You can use the money you saved to invest in staff development and quality software. However, if the operating system is esoteric or obsolete, you will have nothing but headaches. Currently available printers and software will probably work only intermittently, or not work at all. Your enthusiasm and excitement will diminish and you'll face frustration and doubt about the value of computers as tools for learning.

One additional comment related to software and printing is relevant here. Reviewing educational software for classroom use directly ties to the availability of the print option. Generally, if the software does not give children the opportunity to print their creations or their computer work, it can be considered of questionable value in supporting early literacy experiences.

CONSIDER THIS

Efforts should be made to ensure access to appropriate technology for children with special needs, for whom assistive technologies may be essential for successful inclusion (NAEYC, 1996). Federal laws require that students with special needs receive their education in the least restrictive environment (LRE) possible. Full inclusion requires teachers to make adaptations to their curriculum, methods, and materials (including technology).

Accommodating Students with Special Needs

Consider possible types of adaptations that can provide accommodation for students with special needs before you purchase computer components. Technological innovations can help teachers "level the playing field" for these students and enable them to succeed in general education classrooms. We'll briefly look at this idea of including all students in the learning process and how computers can be supportive. First is a discussion of the types of students who generally require assistive devices, followed by considerations of how computers as assistive devices may enable students with disabilities to become active learners in general education classrooms.

Students with visible physical limitations (including those with visual impairments/blindness and hearing impairments/deafness) seem to be those who most frequently use computers as assistive or communication devices to support their learning. However, students with cognitive impairments can also benefit from the use of the computer as an assistive device.

For example, the notion of using the computer as an assistive device expands when students with mental impairments use the computer to practice concept mastery through repetition of material. Students with learning disabilities may have perceptual and visual motor problems that result in impaired learning, and they benefit from assistive use of computers. Some students with physical and learning disabilities have great difficulty writing manually and employ word processing to help them complete assignments that require a written product. Using the keyboard and mouse as input devices provides the kinesthetic sensory stimulation that assists these children in learning.

Technological accommodations can be categorized according to the following: (1) adaptive peripherals, (2) operating system accessibility options, (3) modifications of software, and (4) peer-assisted adaptations.

Adaptive peripherals are generally special switches or hardware devices that plug into the central processing unit or keyboard port and provide an alternative to using the keyboard or mouse as an input device.

Operating system accessibility options relate to the keyboard, mouse, and video display. They may be simple adjustments that can be set in the operating system and then are immediately available for all software access by that particular student. In such cases, in addition to matching the user's special needs for access, the transparency of the adaptation or modification is the key goal. Children with special needs in inclusive classrooms do not want to be singled out from their nondisabled peers any more than is necessary. The more closely the technology enhancements reflect the "norm," the more readily acceptable it is to educators and students. The goal of transparency paves the way for universally designed access for all users in all technology-based products.

Software modifications may be necessary in the case of children with communication impairments, especially in the area of expressive language function. For example, a software program designed specifically to meet the needs of these learners offers a visual scan of choices so the student with a pointing device can simply nod when the desired option is highlighted. Rather than purchasing a product designed for each sensory impairment, select software with teacher tools that permit the teacher to create modifications of software activities to accommodate the special needs of individual learners or small groups of students.

Peer-assisted adaptations involve grouping students and using peers as tutors or partners to assist those with special needs. Carefully implement this option and give equal consideration to the needs of the "helper" and the child with special needs.

CONSIDER THIS

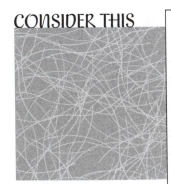

Early childhood educators should use technology as a tool for communication and collaboration among professionals as well as a tool for teaching children (NAEYC, 1996). Use of the Internet is quickly evolving as an important way to connect educators in different locations across the country and around the world. It provides access to national, state, and local curriculum standards.

Internet Access

Internet access is quickly evolving as an important way to increase communication and collaboration among teachers and as a vehicle for staff development. In order to support access to the Internet, you will need a modem. The most critical feature of a modem is the speed of accessing the information bits (parts of an information unit). Higher-speed modems of 1.6 bits per second (bps) enable quicker downloads from and uploads to the Internet. However, your actual opportunity to use this capacity can be limited by the size of the "pipe" transmitting your information, graphics, and sound files. These communication models are continually changing, increasing speed and capacity. Although you may hear about a particular model, check to see if it is available in your local community.

Wireless is becoming more popular for Internet as well as keyboard and mouse input. This option does not require an actual physical connection to either the computer or phone line. Wireless units can facilitate mouse and keyboard use for young children by permitting flexibility in positioning the input device without the interference of the cable that attaches it to the computer. The downside is that without the physical connection, either of these input devices could "walk" away from the computer area and be lost within other areas of the classroom, thus prohibiting use by anyone.

Your computer screen may show an icon for the Internet, but this does not necessarily mean you can simply "double-click" and go there. This icon usually indicates that the system is "Internet ready." Generally unless your computer has been enabled with the modem, cable, Internet subscription service, and so on, you won't be able to access the Internet.

Service Contracts and Warranties

Warranties and on-site service are important considerations. Purchasing a PC from a major manufacturer is more likely to ensure that all component parts have the same time frame for warranty and service support. If you purchase from a local hardware vendor that combines parts from a variety of suppliers, it is essential for you to question specifically the warranty provisions and service costs for each component. Avoid assuming that all parts are under the same warranty and service provisions. For example, a monitor may have a one-year warranty for parts but only a three-month replacement provision. In this case if problems occur beyond the three-month period, you may have to return the monitor to the computer vendor for repair and pay labor costs. There is no charge for replacement parts. Also, you may wonder how long it will take to repair the monitor. Is there a "loaner" monitor provided in the meantime while yours is getting the warranty work completed?

Take care to determine the exact nature of warranties and on-site or "carry-in" service provisions. These are just like they sound. With on-site service, the vendor sends a technician to your classroom to fix the problem. With "carry-in" options you are required to bring the unit or nonfunctioning hardware into the computer dealer for diagnosis and repair or replacement.

Networks

Computer networks are emerging as options for many educational facilities. This section discusses some of the key terms and issues related to computer networking. Let's start at the beginning.

A network is two or more computers connected by some type of communication medium (e.g., cable or infrared signal). A network computer workstation exists in contrast to a stand-alone computer that is not connected to any other computer. In a network environment the attached computers can share printers, other peripherals, data files, and software applications. With stand-alone computers all of these must be directly attached to the computer, reside on the hard disk, or be accessed from diskette, CD-ROM, or the Internet. Remember, each computer, whether it is a workstation on a network or a stand-alone, requires the software operating system. Without an operating system installed, the computer cannot access any software applications and, hence, is a useless machine.

Within the concept of networking there are more than one option: peer-to-peer networking and client-server networking. In the peer-to-peer option, two or more computers are connected and may share some, all, or none of their files. All computers in this type of arrangement are equal and all computers are used as workstations. The Windows operating system offers software that supports this type of networking reliably and effectively. Twenty to thirty computers with two or more printers can use this type of peer-to-peer networking option successfully.

The client-server network requires special networking software and the designation of one computer as the "server." This server computer can be a file server, e-mail server, or print server and all the other computers on the network are workstations or "clients." The server is usually a high-end PC often with several processors and not generally used as a workstation. The server is dedicated to the job of managing the process of sharing and accessing resources across all the workstations. In a large network hundreds of workstations can be connected to several server computers. These types of networks probably require a full-time network administrator to support and maintain the operation.

Benefits of using a network include file sharing and the option to access any software from any workstation at any time. This can be particularly desirable in school settings where instructional requirements to individualize are important. For example, regardless of a student's grade or classroom assignment, software designed for his or her instructional needs is available and easily accessed from the file server.

The downside is that networks require an individual with specialized training and experience to administer the system efficiently and effectively. Usually this means a network administrator is on-site or almost immediately available in the event of hardware or software problems that might arise. When problems occur with the server, it frequently means that every software application and every workstation attached to the network goes "down" and that's an emergency!

Many computer hardware manufacturers and dealers "bundle" software with their computer offerings. These free software bundles are frequently limited editions of brand-name programs or dated second-shelf titles that had limited sales when introduced. Avoid buying a computer based on the bundled software package. And do not believe the claims of "$1,500 worth of free software." Many "free" titles require you to continue a paid subscription after the initial free time expires (e.g., Internet service). Those same free Internet offers are usually available to the general public from the source of the service anyway.

Free software bundles have two consequences. They divert your attention from selecting the hardware configuration that you really need and delay software decisions that are critically important to the educational use of the system. Remember the discussion in which we recommended that you select the software first because this decision dictates your hardware requirements? Bundled packages cloud the issue of selecting quality software. Getting lots of "free software" does a disservice to your achieving your educational goals and selecting quality software for classroom computers. Once you have this bundle you are tempted to allow the children to use it without applying the thoughtful criteria you have developed (see Chapter 2, "Selecting Quality Software"). Sure, poor quality software won't "hurt" children, but why waste their time when you could do better?

Furniture

Finally, after the hardware and peripherals are determined, we need to consider furniture. We recommend that you give special consideration to the furniture that you will use with the equipment in your classroom. Be sure that the furniture is sturdy and has plenty of space to allow you to comfortably arrange all of the system components. The height of the furniture should be suitable so young children can work comfortably when seated. Be sure there is no glare on the screen. While you are positioning the monitor, look at the screen from the child's height when checking for glare.

Experience has shown us that unless resources are allocated to acquire and set up appropriate furniture, the results are invariably frustrating for both the teacher and the children. The correct equipment properly set up makes it easy for the children to select and use the equipment independently. Allocating sufficient space will enable you to monitor the equipment function and use easily.

What works best depends on the space available in your classroom and the security of your facility. If you have a fairly secure site, then you needn't worry about having computers that fit into locking cabinets and roll into a secure area for weekend storage. However, if you are concerned about theft, or if you share space with a group of children who use your classroom after hours or on Sundays, you might consider such furniture.

The challenge is finding furniture that not only meets your security needs but also facilitates children's use. To ensure partners can effectively use the computer, the screen should be visible for more than just the child sitting directly in front of the computer. Often rich interactions occur around the computer when passersby stop to comment or engage in conversations with those partners using the computer. For this reason putting the computer in a locking cabinet that limits screen visibility by others is not advised.

Without security issues as a primary concern, consider using widely available primary size tables and chairs. A standard 5-foot long table (18 inches high) is of sufficient size to easily accommodate an entire computer setup with a CPU, speakers, mouse, keyboard, and a printer. Sometimes two computers share a printer through a switch box. This saves the space that an extra printer would require. Be sure that the table fits against a wall with an outlet and that the arrangement of the equipment facilitates children's independent use, especially with respect to retrieving

printouts. We recommend a multioutlet surge protector that permits you to plug in all your electrical cords. This makes it convenient to turn the computer on and off with a single switch. With a single switch to turn the system on and off, you won't have to worry about whether the speakers were turned off when you left for the day.

You might consider being able to move the computer setup to a larger space so you and a small group of children could use the computer together. This enables you to introduce new software, review and reflect on procedures children have used, or write group stories with more than two children. In this case rollers or wheels might make such use convenient.

To help prevent theft, think about simply locking down the central processing unit (CPU) as this is the most expensive part of your computer setup. The lock-down option offers more flexibility in terms of maximizing screen visibility and still provides some safety measures.

In the case in which you share classroom space and do not want others accessing your computers, it may be sufficient to unplug and remove the mouse and keyboard from the system unit. This can be a bit of a hassle depending on how easy it is to get to the back of the system unit where these plugs are. Store the mouse and keyboard in a safe place such as a locked cupboard. Removing the input devices makes access to the computer unavailable when your classroom is in use by others. The security of your software and system is maintained. Finding a safe place to store the mouse and keyboard is much easier than relocating and locking up an entire computer setup.

Furthermore, we recommend that you add a rider for replacement computers to your basic insurance policy. Even with the precautions you have taken to ensure the safety and security of your equipment, occasionally equipment is stolen despite your best efforts. Insurance provisions will cover the replacement of the equipment.

Furniture Cautions

We do have a word or two about what we do not recommend when it comes to appropriate furniture. On the market there are several molded, hard plastic units available that incorporate the computer equipment as part of the furniture. The unit comes with a bench for two. Software is preloaded. These units are very "cute," come in primary colors, and seem safely and securely childproof in terms of dangling cords, cables, and so on. Intuitively this kind of computer

Use a computer table that offers screen visibility even for passersby.

setup seems just the way to go—it's easy to purchase, safe and secure, "all in one," and you've satisfied one critical part of the technology equation—getting the computer!

However, on closer examination of the situation we can identify several reasons why this furniture/computer option is *not* optimizing your investment. When we consider technology as a tool, it is a tool not only for the children but for the teaching staff as well. The lack of flexibility of an "all in one unit" does not promote this critical concept.

The "all in one" option not only trivializes the tool nature of the computer for professionals, but it also limits convenient and effective use of the computer by the teaching staff. With all the components permanently installed in the hard case, the ability to adjust the screen and keyboard or use a printer is constrained. Ergonomically the situation can be hazardous for adults.

The height of molded panels encasing the computer setup makes screen visibility limited. This inhibits children not directly using the computer from participation in the computer activity. (*Note:* Such participation enhances the social use of the computer and has positive effects on language development.)

Generally, there is no printer or space to install one conveniently. And as we noted before, how do you support emergent literacy experiences when there is no hard copy that permits you to share what is written or created? Teachers find printing extremely useful for their instructional needs.

In this setup, the disk drive and CD-ROM drive are inaccessible to both children and teachers. Although this protects the system unit from potential damage by exploring "little hands," it also makes it very inconvenient for authorized use by the adults in the classroom. There are always trade-offs when considering the alternatives available. Keep in mind your classroom environment and layout and the age (average size) and characteristics (including impulse control and maturity) of the children you teach.

Finally, the "all in one" unit comes with a price to match. This price is far greater than the sum of the parts. If you purchase computer and furniture components separately (equipment, software, and furniture), you will have funds remaining for buying quality software for teachers and children. Selecting this "cute" and convenient option means that you have sacrificed about half of the capacity of the computer to make a difference in the early education classroom. Again, we return to the focus at the beginning of chapter—what are your goals for acquiring technology in your program?

Troubleshooting

Solving problems that arise at the computer does not always require extensive technical knowledge. Often applying common sense and approaching the problem in a systematic, patient, and calm manner can solve these problems.

We have found that a variety of malfunctions can be traced to a group of commonly occurring causes. Generally, there could be two kinds of problems that arise: hardware and/or software. Often it is difficult for the new user to determine which type of problem is occurring. All you know is that you or the children can't get into the programs or use the computer the way you usually do, and this is frustrating!

If there is a message on the screen, write it down exactly. Later you may need to tell a tech support person what you read, and that needs to be exact. If the message advises you to do something, follow that direction. If the problem is not resolved, then turn off the computer.

As a first step in determining the possible cause, check all of the electrical and system unit connections including the surge suppressor and wall outlet. Check the monitor, keyboard, mouse, and printer plugs, cords, and cables. Be sure they are all firmly connected to ensure they are getting power. A common cause of computer problems, even with adults, is a plug that is not securely attached.

Now that all connections are secure, turn on the computer again. If it appears that one of the components is still not working, you may want to substitute a component you know is working from another setup. This will help you isolate the problem.

Write down what happens according to what you see on the screen or hear from the system unit. If you cannot proceed with any other on-screen suggestions, call your technical support number.

From time to time you may have heard about computer viruses that damage the data stored on the computer. A computer virus can cause a variety of problems that do not respond to the basic troubleshooting remedies. Viruses can be transmitted to your computer via the Internet or from diskettes you receive from other users. Protecting your system from viruses is a good reason not to share software with others. A variety of virus software packages are available to help protect your system. However, the main reason for not sharing software is due to copyright and licensing restrictions. This also turns out to be a good reason to discourage parents or colleagues from loaning home software to the classroom.

Summary Points

- Selecting hardware and system components for the early childhood classroom relates to the software you have selected.
- The "life span" of a computer system is generally one to three years.

- Maintenance and hardware support contracts are a "must" to help ensure effective classroom use by early childhood educators.
- Appropriate furniture facilitates integration and effective use of classroom computers.

What's Next?

Now that you have become familiar with the components necessary to set up a computer learning center in your classroom, you are ready to think about how to implement the concept of using computers. The next chapter offers detailed descriptions of the computer learning center setup and specific ideas of how to introduce computers to young children.

Apply Your Learning

1. Make a shopping list of the hardware and peripherals you need to purchase to set up your classroom computer(s). The partially completed sample chart will help you get started.

Item	Minimum Requirements	Maximum Requirements	Warranty	Costs
CPU				
Hard drive				
Memory (RAM)				
Furniture				

2. Identify hardware sources for items on your list. Use the Yellow Pages or local phone book and recommendations from colleagues or the Internet. Select three or four sources and record names and phone numbers. Contact each source and complete the chart you've developed.

Company Name	Phone Number	Comments
1.		
2.		
3.		

3. Compare prices and services. Consider the pros and cons.

Company Name	Pros	Cons
1.		
2.		
3.		

4. Call the toll-free support number for each company. Confirm that the number is not just for ordering, but also that you can receive technical support (or find out how that is handled). Write comments about your results.

_____

_____

_____

5. Evaluate your results. Decide which vendors offer you the highest-quality products and services for a fair price. Consider convenience in terms of ordering, delivery, setup, and staff in-service training. Document your results.

_____

_____

_____

6. The following chart permits you to organize and monitor your hardware acquisition and installation process. Begin with information gathering and end with implementing in-service training. Complete it for your school or center.

COMPUTER SYSTEM IMPLEMENTATION PLANNING DOCUMENT

Goals:

Participants:

Time Frame:

Tasks	Person Responsible	Action Steps	Completion Date

Setting Up and Introducing the Classroom Computer

Before you begin using technology with young children, you must determine where to locate your computers, how to connect the different parts, set guidelines for use, and introduce these tools to youngsters. This chapter discusses these issues whether you locate computers in your classroom, a computer lab, or on a rolling cart. We address tasks that may appear simple to some but complex to others. Good luck as you continue the adventure.

Teachers Ask

▶ *What is the best way to organize computers?*

Placing computers in the classroom allows teachers to more easily integrate them into the curriculum (NAEYC, 1996). Computers, complete with printers, become one of many learning centers or workstations children use.

▶ *How many children can use the computer at one time?*

At minimum, two children may use one computer simultaneously. One child actually uses the mouse or keyboard while the other acts as an observing partner. This combination promotes socioemotional, language, and cognitive development (Clements & Samara, 2002; Haugland & Shade, 1990). Additionally children initiate more and different types of interactions when working together (NAEYC, 1996).

▶ *How much time should young children spend with computers?*

After the introductory period, allow children to self-limit their time at the computer center as they do at other learning centers. Ensure that *all* classroom learning materials and activities are engaging and intellectually stimulating.

After Reading This Chapter, You'll Know

- How to arrange the computer learning center.
- How to connect the various computer components.
- How to introduce the computer learning center to young children.
- How child-initiated activity can be supported with technology.
- Where to put your computer learning center.
- How to avoid common mistakes when organizing or introducing the computer center.

Organizing the Classroom Computer Learning Center

In your classroom with twenty or fewer children, two computers and a shared printer provide sufficient resources for a learning center setup. This computer learning center arrangement offers maximum opportunities for most preschool and kindergarten groups (MOBIUS, 1994). That's a ratio of one computer to ten children. As older children begin to use computers for writing, research, project work, and skill building, we recommend additional hardware, perhaps three to five computers for the average class of twenty-five to thirty students.

Ideally for preschool classrooms, each computer learning center has two computers and one printer. (One computer per ten children is an adequate ratio.) Increase the number of computers as children use them more effectively for writing and research. When you plan, expect two children to use each computer. Therefore, at minimum, four children participate at the computer learning center when two computers are available. If you can only afford one computer in your preschool learning center, you can expect to provide closer supervision as children may compete aggressively for the limited resource of computer time.

You must consider two issues when organizing computer materials and equipment in your classroom. The first is the actual location of the learning center and the second is the organization of the equipment within the learning center.

Classroom Computer Center Location

As early childhood educators learn about child development, curriculum, and assessment, they also discover how the organization of the physical environment can maximize children's learning. The broad guidelines for organizing space remain the same no matter what curriculum you follow. Let's review them here and then apply them to the computer center setup.

- Place related centers adjacent to each other; include materials that enhance each area.
- Avoid placing quiet centers next to noisy ones.
- Make certain that safety and physical needs are met (electricity/traffic patterns, appropriate-sized furniture and space).
- Plan sufficient space to allow children to work cooperatively.
- Be sure that materials offer a variety of multisensory and developmental experiences.
- Use child-sized furniture to facilitate learning.
- Arrange materials in a way that encourages children to assume some responsibility for maintaining the environment.

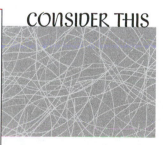

CONSIDER THIS

Locating computers in the classroom makes them easily accessible. Children and teachers can then use computers as one of many classroom learning tools as well as enhance their integration with other curriculum activities (NAEYC, 1996). Locating computers in a lab situation or on a rolling cart, however, is workable.

Obviously, the broad guidelines for the computer learning center are similar to those of other learning centers. However, there are some critical differences and special requirements. The computer center should exist in a well-defined space that reflects the following considerations. (The same factors apply if your computers are in a lab or on a rolling cart. Look for specific issues about these locations near the end of this chapter.)

Safety.   Place the computers against a wall with an electrical outlet easily accessible. This location will prevent the children from tripping over the numerous power cords and cables required by the computer and printer setup. Some manufacturers design computer furniture with storage for the cables and cords. This is almost essential if you cannot place your learning center against a wall.

Equipment Care.   Keep materials such as paint, water, sand, and food away from your computers. If spilled, these materials may be harmful to the operation of the computer. Because the computer software programs are stored on magnetic media (disks) and proximity to a magnet can damage the software, magnets can be another source of concern. Magnets are not always as obvious as those we use in the science center so be on the lookout.

Lighting.   Place your computers to avoid glare from the sun coming through the windows or the overhead lights. To check for glare on the computer monitor screen, sit in the child's chair and look at the screen from the child's height. Several manufacturers offer screen glare guards that you place on the monitor to reduce this problem. Generally these guards are relatively inexpensive.

Integrate computers with other classroom learning centers.

*G*etting the printout can also serve as an indicator that the child's turn is completed. Now it's the partner's turn.

Traffic Patterns. The prevalent placement for the computer is away from direct traffic; however, some teachers find it easier to integrate the computer with other learning centers if it is more centrally located. This central location offers passersby a chance to comment on what the partners are doing at the computers. Use whichever style seems more suitable to your curriculum and personal preference.

Noise Level. There is often some need to place the computers away from noisy classroom activities due to the essential voice support young children require. Noisy activities may interfere with children hearing the voiced feedback and instructions from the computer. Be careful, too, that the computer feedback, music, and audio don't disturb children who are trying to engage in a quiet activity, such as book reading. (If needed, use headphones for the computer center to eliminate computer-generated noise. Most systems come equipped for this option.) Sometimes teachers make the computer part of the writing center or even the dramatic play center. It becomes a flexible tool that allows the dramatic center to become an office, library, or restaurant. Children can create and print letters, messages, menus, and so on. Offering the computer in such contexts underscores this medium as a tool that provides children meaningful play opportunities for integration of ideas about their world with technology.

Review the chart in Figure 4.1 to help you choose the best space in your classroom for your computer center. Before you start, draw a map of your classroom that includes the placement of doors, windows, electrical outlets, sinks, and other learning centers with potential hazards, such as water and sand.

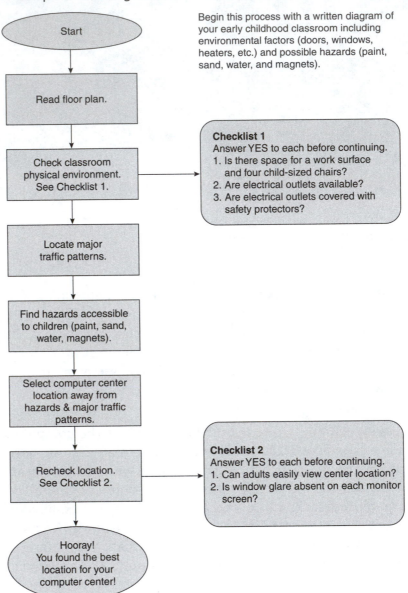

Figure 4.1 How to Select a Classroom Location for the Computer Learning Center

Begin this process with a written diagram of your early childhood classroom including environmental factors (doors, windows, heaters, etc.) and possible hazards (paint, sand, water, and magnets).

Start

Read floor plan.

Check classroom physical environment. See Checklist 1.

Checklist 1
Answer YES to each before continuing.
1. Is there space for a work surface and four child-sized chairs?
2. Are electrical outlets available?
3. Are electrical outlets covered with safety protectors?

Locate major traffic patterns.

Find hazards accessible to children (paint, sand, water, magnets).

Select computer center location away from hazards & major traffic patterns.

Recheck location. See Checklist 2.

Checklist 2
Answer YES to each before continuing.
1. Can adults easily view center location?
2. Is window glare absent on each monitor screen?

Hooray! You found the best location for your computer center!

Printer Location. The printer must be visible and accessible to the children. Keep it within the children's safe reach, whether they are sitting or standing. Easy access to the printer helps children independently retrieve completed printouts.

Printing a picture takes time. When a child can watch as the printer processes his or her screen image into hard copy, it makes the waiting time manageable. This process fascinates children. One minute an image is on the computer screen, and shortly it is printed on a piece a paper, ready for displaying in the classroom or sharing with family and friends at home.

If children cannot watch their pictures printing, they may not realize that they are actually in control of the print function. The ability to see what's going on with the printer focuses children's attention while they wait for the computer to become available for their use again.

An additional important aspect of printing is that it can aid the child in reflecting on the processes he or she used at the computer. The printout serves as a visual cue for assisting the child in recalling and verbalizing the procedures he or she used at the computer to create the output. Debriefing about computer experiences assists the children in connecting those experiences with other hands-on learning.

Furniture. Selecting appropriate furniture is more complicated than it may appear. As educators, we see a table and printer stand that fit exactly our notion of what a computer learning center should look like: cute, child-sized chairs, colorful and sturdy table, a place to store wires and cables, and about the right height for your children. But wait! Buy furniture *after* you measure your monitor and computer components. Are they separate units? How many computers will you have at the center? Do you have the option of storing the processor unit either horizontally or vertically? If so, will each part operate correctly? Find the answer to these questions, especially if someone else is ordering the computers or furniture.

Use the following chart as a guideline for the furniture that you will need. Nothing is more frustrating than having to wait while someone returns the chair or table you *thought* was the correct size. Do you plan to use the computers for both adults and children in a family literacy environment? If so, the height of the table should be easily adjustable and, possibly, the entire unit should be mobile.

COMMON DIMENSIONS OF COMPUTER UNITS

	1 Computer	2 Computers
Length	36 inches	72 inches
Width	24–28 inches	24–28 inches
Height	22–30 inches	22–30 inches

Here's what happened at one center where the teachers and director thought they had carefully considered all factors related to computer furniture. They selected furniture that supported positioning the computer screen so that it was flush with the tabletop. Intuitively, this seemed like a good idea. Children could sit at the table and easily view the screen. They could move the mouse in relation to the parallel position of the screen and become accustomed more readily to controlling the mouse. Under the table was a shelf for vertically storing the computer system unit itself. It wouldn't take up space on the tabletop. Although these attributes of the furniture made sense, when the computer arrived, the teachers found that the system unit could not be stored vertically because it interfered with the operation of the CD-ROM drive. In this particular computer system unit the CD-ROM had to be inserted horizontally in order to work.

Although relatively new, the field of computer ergonomics for children is also important to consider. Experts suggest the following guidelines when using computers with children (Fryer, 1999).

1. Make sure that the monitor is at the child's eye level.
2. Use an adjustable chair so the child's forearms and wrists are parallel to the floor.
3. Place the monitor so the child's head is 16 to 24 inches from the screen.
4. Install keyboard trays so arms bend comfortably at a 90-degree angle (whether using the keyboard or a mouse).

Security.   Is security an issue? If so, does this furniture arrangement facilitate bolting down the hardware? Have you considered where you'll store related computer materials and equipment? Is there a built-in cover that you can close and lock? Computer furniture often incorporates a locking cabinet that facilitates storing the keyboard, mouse, and other peripherals. A thief may not be as interested if he or she cannot get everything for an entire setup. Sometimes just throwing a sheet over the entire learning center suffices as a security precaution and keeps weekend dust and dirt away from the equipment. Many programs share facilities over the weekend for church or another organization's activities. The computer center becomes an inviting attraction. In these cases, it is best to move the entire computer center to a locked room or closet. Be certain that your furniture has wheels that easily support such a move.

Where Do All Those Wires Go?

Many computer systems today arrive with color-coded cords and icons to indicate which wires connect to which outlet. Manufacturers also include very specific instructions for assembling computer systems. Hardware manufacturers work diligently to write clear manuals and directions, but even with these aids, you might encounter difficulty, especially if you have several peripherals to attach.

Probably one of the most challenging and possibly confusing scenarios for beginners is the actual connection of the various computer components. (See Figure 4.2.) The sight of all the cables, plugs, cords, and electrical contraptions piled on the table with the monitor, system unit, mouse, keyboard, printer, and so on is enough to send an otherwise mature and competent adult screaming from the room. There appears to be no logical or rational explanation for how all the parts and pieces go together to make a congruent whole. Besides, most early childhood educators are more high touch than high tech. We are more inclined to understand how people (children, in particular) work as opposed to how mechanical and elec-

Figure 4.2   Connecting Your Computer Components, Printer, and Switch Box

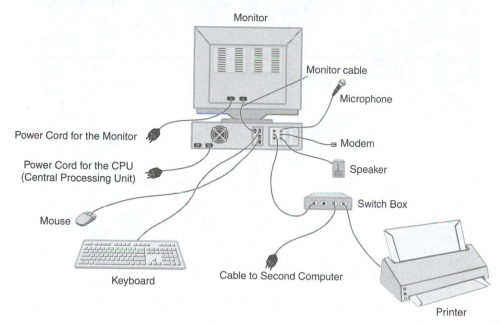

trical parts go together. We are those adults who dread an electrical storm that sets every digital clock on every home appliance blinking for our attention, demanding we consult the operating manual to reset the time.

All those wires with funny-shaped ends can be intimidating even for the strongest hearts. Relax. We have answers. The process is just about as simple as a child's matching game. Even very young children quickly learn that a square peg, no matter how hard you push, will not fit easily into a round hole.

The Two Rules of Connecting

There are two general rules. Rule 1: Each connection has a matched partner that will fit together with it snugly. If for some reason, you have difficulty in connecting two pieces, remember rule 1. If you find the perfect partner for your connection, they will go together easily.

Rule 2: If you believe you have found a match according to rule 1, but it doesn't readily go together without major pushing, prodding, or forcing, avoid great strength, a bigger hammer, the bodybuilder next door, and any other forms of chutzpah, grits, or guts. *Do not force any connection.* Trying to make something fit to the wrong partner is like trying to force the plug for a floor lamp into your car's cigarette lighter. You might be able to plug them together. However, once made, the connection will not enable either the lamp or the lighter to work properly and will probably damage *both*.

Be aware that violating either of these basic rules could result in expensive repairs. This is one of the few times you can really be responsible for serious damage to your computer and its related parts. Enough said.

*V*arious computer components can be confusing, especially to the novice user.

Sort all cables according to the types of connection ends before you actually start to hook anything together. Begin with the longest cable and attach it to the matching hole (called *port* in tech-talk) at the back of the computer. If you cannot readily determine the match between cable and port through visual inspection, use a trial-and-error process to proceed. Remember: (1) There is a match and (2) be gentle. Once you find the match, be sure the thumbscrews are snugly tightened. You may need a screwdriver to do this. The key words here are "careful" and "gentle." The screws are quite tiny so use a little screwdriver like the type you might use to repair a sewing machine or pair of eyeglasses. Avoid tightening thumbscrews too tightly because this could strip the screws and make them ineffective.

Many computers have a power cord that must be plugged into the monitor and another one that is plugged into the system unit before both of these are plugged into a surge protector. "What's a surge protector?" you ask. Well, the computer is especially sensitive to spikes and surges in electrical power, so a special box is used to help control the flow of electricity to the computer. The power cords from the computer, monitor, and printer are plugged into the surge protector and then the surge protector is plugged into the wall outlet. This device protects your computer from electrical brown-outs and power surges that can accompany thunderstorms. It also can be convenient by having one on/off switch for all your computer components.

See Figure 4.3 for step-by-step procedures for connecting the components and peripherals of your computer center. With the hands-on assembly of your computer learning center, you have started a journey that will

Figure 4.3 How to Assemble a Computer Center

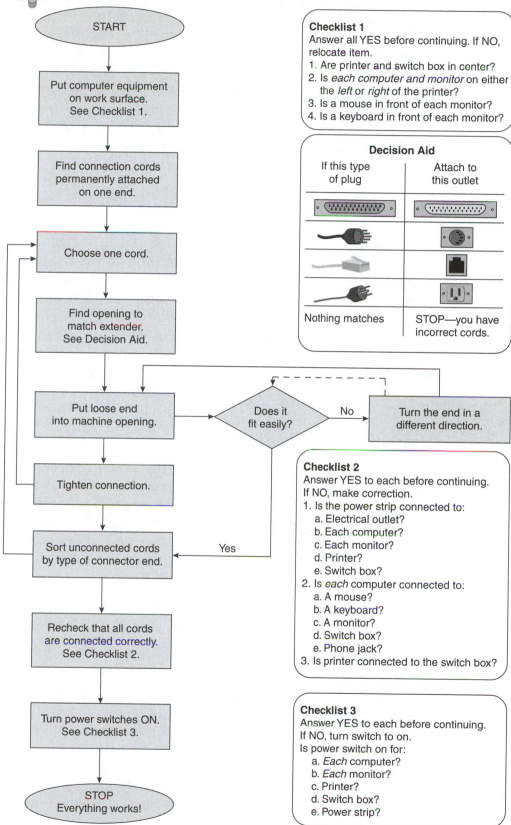

START

Put computer equipment
on work surface.
See Checklist 1.

Find connection cords
permanently attached
on one end.

Choose one cord.

Find opening to
match extender.
See Decision Aid.

Put loose end
into machine opening.

Does it
fit easily?

No → Turn the end in a
different direction.

Tighten connection.

Sort unconnected cords
by type of connector end.

Yes

Recheck that all cords
are connected correctly.
See Checklist 2.

Turn power switches ON.
See Checklist 3.

STOP
Everything works!

Checklist 1
Answer all YES before continuing. If NO,
relocate item.
1. Are printer and switch box in center?
2. Is *each computer and monitor* on either
   the *left* or *right* of the printer?
3. Is a mouse in front of each monitor?
4. Is a keyboard in front of each monitor?

Decision Aid

If this type of plug	Attach to this outlet
Nothing matches	STOP—you have incorrect cords.

Checklist 2
Answer YES to each before continuing.
If NO, make correction.
1. Is the power strip connected to:
   a. Electrical outlet?
   b. Each computer?
   c. Each monitor?
   d. Printer?
   e. Switch box?
2. Is *each* computer connected to:
   a. A mouse?
   b. A keyboard?
   c. A monitor?
   d. Switch box?
   e. Phone jack?
3. Is printer connected to the switch box?

Checklist 3
Answer YES to each before continuing.
If NO, turn switch to on.
Is power switch on for:
   a. *Each* computer?
   b. *Each* monitor?
   c. Printer?
   d. Switch box?
   e. Power strip?

ultimately lead you to the "power up" stage, where you actually turn on the computer and its little lights flash! You can now celebrate your success.

When teachers have a chance to unpack and set up the computer hardware and related equipment, they feel more in control of the technology. It is an experience that demystifies the technology, so to speak. As a result, teachers become much more comfortable troubleshooting and ensuring, for example, that cables are snugly connected so the printer gets power. Once teachers have successfully assembled the computers and printer, they won't be intimidated about packing up for the summer or moving the computer center to another part of the classroom if the initial placement does not work as planned.

Introducing Computers to Children

The children in your classroom may have various degrees of computer experience. Your introduction to computers will differ based on how much your students already know. Conduct an informal assessment with children before you begin. Determine how many students are skilled with using a mouse, keyboard, and other facets of computer operation. What types of software programs have children used? Were they primarily games or open-ended programs? Can they operate input devices independently and with skill? Use the answers to these questions and the following strategies to plan effective and engaging introduction activities.

Preschool and Kindergarten

Introduce technology to your class using the same strategies and activities you use with any other new learning medium or experience. Although the computer is electronic, automatic, and advertised as "user friendly," you must pay attention and offer children clear instruction in its care and use. Remember when you introduced easel painting? You offered only one or two paint colors at a time and explained that the brush for red only goes in the red paint container. You also probably demonstrated cleanup by wiping the brushes on all sides before taking them in a bucket to the sink to wash. You'll want to develop step-by-step directions for the use of computers in the same manner.

Introduce computers and software to young children in the way you would any other new material or activity. Often educators use small groups or circle time as demonstration and explanation periods. If possible, expand the computer screen images on a large-screen TV or computer monitor. Then demonstrate some of the functions and features of the software. Using a television as a monitor requires that you use a special connection purchased separately; however, with this larger screen, you can introduce the computer to a group of children (about half your class at one time). This will speed up the process of getting the children ready for independent use of the computer.

In a small group the teacher introduces and demonstrates how to use a new software program.

In small groups the teacher introduces the computer as a vehicle for taking dictation of group stories. This provides children with a context for computer use. It allows children to see their teacher use the computer as a tool. Furthermore, such a demonstration establishes the importance of some early literacy concepts; for example, print is a written down, left to right, and top to bottom display of text, and print is meaningful. Obviously, this strategy is not effective for software games.

As each child takes a turn, the teacher types in the statements and the screen displays the written text. A printout of the final story or narrative is made for each child. A copy of the story can be posted on the bulletin board. Introducing the computer this way provides children a model for their own writing process. They'll become interested in exploring the use of the keyboard to produce letters on the screen, then words, and soon their own stories. So essentially there are three easy steps: (1) Help the children make something, (2) print it, and (3) hang it up.

Explaining How a Computer Works

There is a tendency for some early childhood educators to provide either insufficient or absolutely huge amounts of information to children about how the computer works. Remember to tailor your explanation to the developmental level of the children. Just as you don't expect to give detailed descriptions of the workings of the telephone or microwave; neither should you do this about the computer. Therefore, keep your explanation simple.

We tend to favor the explanation of the computer as another tool that people use to help them work. This tool needs electricity to work. All of the parts must be connected so that each can receive power. (There is no need at this point to explain electricity.) You can use energy as an alternative and provide examples of cars needing gas to run, people needing food for energy, and computers needing electricity to run.

Once the computer has power, it is critical for children to understand that it is a machine designed and built by people; it is not magic. The computer will do what we want because of instructions people have given it. There is no little person inside the machine. In many ways it is similar to a tape recorder or CD player. Neither by itself creates music. Someone puts the music on a cassette or CD and when this is placed inside the player music comes out.

If you work with young children, it may be useful for you to show a disk, cassette tape, and a record or CD to illustrate that these all have similar purposes. You can insert a CD into a computer just like you would insert a tape into a cassette player. CDs (or disks, depending on your software) provide the concrete example of how people provide information that the computer can "read."

Using CD-ROM media for actually loading the software programs may create another problem. We believe that often it is preferable for an adult to load the software onto the computer hard drive. While the computer is "loading," children waiting for the right time to insert the CD may accidentally damage it. You may find fingerprints, crayon, or even peanut butter smears on this magnetic medium. So to avoid this issue, load all software programs onto your hard drive.

The CD-ROM drive opening itself is also intriguing to young children. Even with careful directions about the importance of only CDs being placed here, teachers have found small plastic car parts and even a heart-shaped attribute block inside the drive. Obviously, this creates serious problems. Children observe that there is an opening and sometimes adults put things inside. It is part of their natural curiosity and experimentation; however, it is not something that you want to encourage with this particular part of the computer center.

Next, two early childhood educators share their success stories and practical strategies for introducing computers to young children in preschool. Both gave their students concrete examples based on the children's previous experiences and practice before using the computer itself. Wendy uses a modified version of the project approach (Katz & Chard, 1989). She helps children who are in the phenomenological make-believe stage of development and do not really understand the abstract concepts underlying computer operation (Turkle, 1984).

Wendy Nashid Makes a Computer

Wendy Nashid is the director of Rise-n-Shine, a home-based learning center for children ages 2 to 8 years old. She designed her child care program to develop the child's natural abilities, self-esteem, and independence. The following describes how she helped her children become "computer ready."

Wendy says, "Computers became the theme of my setting. At circle time we began talking about computers—What are they? Where are they? How do they work? How do you care for them? How much do they cost? How can children use them?"

Preparation.   We took trips to the computer store as if we are going to buy one. We took lots of pictures and documented our experiences on video. We talked about the parts of the computer and what they do. We talked about how to buy a computer, the cost, how to pay—with cash, check, or charge card—how to communicate with the salesperson, and the salesperson's job. We looked at software.

We took trips around the neighborhood to offices, stores, city buildings, and homes with computers. The children asked several questions, such as "Where is your mouse that you need to move to get where you want to go?" Sometimes they even got to touch the computers we saw. They began to recognize different computer parts. We took trips to the library to look for books about computers. We told stories—what I like about computers; what I can do with a computer; if I were a computer.

Soon I felt that the children were immersed in computers. The concept of a computer meant something to the children, but what, I wondered? Were they really ready for a real computer? Would they be gentle? Did they understand the functions of the keyboard, mouse, and so on? Can we practice hands-on learning without destroying the computer? Somehow, I felt we needed more experiences with the idea of having a computer to use in our center, but how could we do this without a real computer available? The only thing I could think of was to create a make-believe computer.

Assembling the Make-Believe Computer.   We talked about what we would need to make a pretend computer. We got boxes of different sizes, cut an opening in one box for the screen, made different computer parts, added cord for cables, assembled the make-believe components, and labeled the creation "Computer."

Our make-believe mouse was a green pepper from the housekeeping area, covered with aluminum foil. At one end of the green pepper, we attached a pipe cleaner. On the other end was an arrow-shaped, pointed cutout of orange poster board. My objective was to get the children to understand how to move the mouse. I used a large loose-leaf notebook as a mouse pad for practicing up-down and side-to-side movements. The mouse buttons serve the same function as the *do it key* (Enter key). We'd say *do it* as they practiced pressing the mouse button while positioning the mouse.

On our pretend screen/monitor, we created a picture by using an 8½" × 11" piece of white paper. Each piece of paper had a different theme picture as if different programs were in use. For example, we had animals, color mixing, shapes, and so on, and a blank paper, so I could put letters and words on it when we composed stories. Children would press the "next key" to move to a new screen or the "see ya' key" to quit. Children could adjust the paper screen in response to the commands.

"Seven Things to Work a Computer" Song.   As we listed the things we need to work the computer, we wrote this song, sung to the tune of "The Farmer in the Dell."

We need seven things to work a computer
Seven things to work a computer;
Tell me what they are.

One is ME,
Two is a disk or CD,
Three is keyboard,
Four is a mouse,
Five is the system unit,
Six is the monitor, and
Seven is the printer!
Now tell me what they do!

I need myself to think about what we want to do,
I use a disk to put the information into the computer,
I use a keyboard to type our work into the computer,
I use the mouse to get somewhere we need to go,
I use the system unit to work everything out,
I use the monitor to see what I'm doing,
I use the printer to print my work!

I know seven things to work a computer,
And I know what they do,
YES!

From Make-Believe to Real.   After much singing and practicing with our make-believe computer, the children were now ready for a real computer. We had a celebration. The children sent invitations to parents and friends to attend a presentation on computers and kids. They shared what they learned through pictures, stories, and video.

The most exciting part was when we brought in a real computer. We reviewed all we'd learned about the computer and how to set up and use the equipment. Finally, we did just that!

Ruth Quigley's Mouse Method

As noted earlier, your children may have various degrees of computer experience. Operating a mouse may be a common skill or something entirely new. (Do you remember your first attempts at trying to put the screen cursor in a particular location?) If you work with preschoolers or kindergartners, try Ruth's Mouse Method. Older children will benefit from a short explanation and demonstration followed by actual practice.

Ruth Quigley, a Head Start teacher, works with 4- and 5-year-olds. She found an effective way of introducing the mouse to children. During circle time she brings a disconnected mouse to the group. She explains how, like a real mouse, it has a tail (the connecting cord to the computer) and two or three buttons that make the computer operate. Ruth places her hand out flat toward the group and asks that they pretend her hand is the mouse. Everyone uses their own hands and practices steering in different directions. She then takes small plastic counting bears and puts them on the carpet in front of her. Ruth explains that she is going to steer her mouse (hand) over the bears and try to pick up the bear. This is like pushing one of the mouse buttons. She continues the explanation by telling the children that once the bear is picked up, they must let it go (e.g., the mouse button is pushed and then released for software that is not "drag and drop"). At the computer, children practice with bears and then with the mouse.

Ruth reminds the children to keep the mouse's tail pointed toward the computer or the cursor won't move in the correct direction. Be certain that your software operates when the mouse button is pressed and then released; some require you to continue to depress the mouse button as you move the cursor around the screen. Your cursor may turn into the object you pick up and be released only when you position that object where you want it on the screen and then release the mouse button. Some mouse units have three buttons with the left and right buttons designated for specific actions within the software, or double-clicks (presses) of the mouse button are required to perform specific actions. For young children software that responds to simple pickup/release mouse use is easier to master.

Some special mouse units are designed to have the mouse cable attached at the "back" of the mouse, so children have an easier time pointing the mouse in the right direction in relation to moving the cursor on the screen. Other manufacturers created mouse variations with large balls or large buttons or special keyboards with keys in alphabetical order to help young children with this process. After some brief instruction and limited practice, most children readily master use of the mouse. Novice teachers encounter the most difficulty and have a hard time believing that children as young as 3 quickly become proficient mouse users. Stand back and watch. Although most every software program for children is "mouse accessible," you may have an old favorite that requires the use of a keyboard. If so, Wendy and Ruth share tips that will help you.

Wendy and Ruth's Keyboard Teaching Tips

Wendy Nashid. When Wendy Nashid teaches children her computer song, she spends more time teaching about the keyboard than other computer parts. Read what Wendy does.

> After showing children that the keyboard has many special keys, I renamed the keys to reflect what they do. Children build understanding when concepts have meaning for them.

We called the Escape key the "see ya " key. I explained that when you want to leave the software program, you press "see ya." We called the Enter key the "do it" key. I told children to use Enter when they have selected something they want to do. We called the spacebar the "next key" because it gets you to the next picture. Finally, I said that the other keys and letters make words (like your name) and these words make stories.

We practiced on our make-believe keyboard with a gentle touch. Children would touch the special keys and recite, "do it, next, and see ya." They would press the keys to spell their names and say the letters out loud. We also played a game in which I called out a letter or key and the children found it on the keyboard. Soon they tried this game with each other. When the functions of the keys were clear to the children, I began to pair our name for the key with the actual keyboard name of the key.

Ruth Quigley.   Ruth uses the correct name for important keys on the keyboard (Escape, Enter, Shift). She combines the appropriate term with a child-friendly definition during her introduction to the keyboard. For example, the Escape key is the "good-bye" key. Ruth stops using the definition as children become accustomed to the key and its use. Ruth suggests using colored stickers to mark the keys. Use red for the key that "stops" or quits the software, green to "go" again (perhaps the C key), and yellow to return to a preceding menu of options (Esc).

Software developers and publishers determine the functions of keys for their programs. Consistency of keyboard commands that supports ease of use may become one of the determining factors in your selections of software appropriate for young children's use.

Primary Grades

Here are additional approaches to use with older children. You may also find the earlier suggestions helpful depending on the composition of your class. Several primary teachers tell us that many first grade children already have had computer experience. Even if a child's family did not have a computer at home, they often had access during preschool or kindergarten. Experienced children, thus, view the computer as a familiar activity. Therefore, when computers are in classrooms, teachers use a general approach and introduce them as they do other curricular materials. Together, teachers and children establish rules for effectively, appropriately, and equitably using the computer center and this becomes the "end of the story." However, if students go to a computer lab, then this experience needs a different set of procedures, mostly because the computers are out of the classroom and down the hall.

Computer labs suggest particular strategies because of their location and the type of software frequently found there. Children often use integrated learning software systems in computer labs that offer explicit curriculum across subject matter areas and practice in isolated skills and concepts. Generally, such integrated software systems track children's progress and monitor further advancement until mastery of particular skills and objectives is achieved. In these cases, teachers must plan activities that help children move from working collaboratively with a partner to solitary practice of skills.

CONSIDER THIS

Integrate technology into the daily routine of classroom activity (NAEYC, 1996). When introducing new functions of hardware or new software programs, use small groups or partner children at the computer for instruction.

Ongoing Use of the Computer Center

At the computer center, use small group activities with four or five children. Each child has a chance to work with a partner and explore functions of the software. Rotate through your class until all children have had a turn.

You might brainstorm with the class some special rules for the computer center. Focus on the positives rather than the "don'ts." You want children to discover that rules for the computer are similar to the rules for the other centers. The guidelines focus on social aspects, such as taking turns and helping others who are less experienced.

Computer Center Rules

1. The computer stays on.
2. Liquids of any kind are off limits in the computer area.
3. Children may use only the controls found on the keyboard or mouse.
4. If you are working in a program and get confused, ask an adult or another child for help.
5. The plastic keyboard cover stays on the keyboard.
6. Only use the mouse (or keyboard) if you are the computer operator.
7. Use gentle hands with the mouse or keyboard.

An illustrated list of procedures using colored symbols helps keep children on track, establishes independent use of the computer, and creates an atmosphere that supports cooperative learning and peer tutoring. A keyboard and mouse command chart is also helpful. Post these charts above the computer center; it helps volunteers and the teacher, too! (See Figure 4.4.)

igure 4.4 Symbols That Help Young Children Use Software Independently

 RED CIRCLE stops

 GREEN CIRCLE clears the screen

 YELLOW CIRCLE exits the program

 TREASURE CHEST with the arrow pointing down saves the child's current picture.

 TREASURE CHEST with the arrow pointing up loads the child's picture, if one was saved.

 FOUR ICONS show the choices available for each category of objects (animals, people, props).

 MICROPHONE allows a sound file to be recorded for any object.

 PRINTER prints whatever part of the farm scene is currently displayed on the screen.

 KEYBOARD loads KIDWARE Writer so that the child can tell a story about what has been created (and printed). An adult can type in the story and then print it for the child.

 EAR repeats the last vocalization (directions or farm animal sounds).

 QUESTION MARK—press this symbol for help (same as F1).

Pair children at the computer to encourage the development of cooperative learning strategies. Use competent peers as computer assistants. They can assist more timid, less risk-taking partners in gaining computer confidence and competence.

Once children have adjusted to the novelty of having a computer center available, the initial competition for turns wears off. Management of the computer is important to consider when children cannot seem to establish a turn-taking routine after the initial novelty period has worn off.

Choose software that appeals to both girls and boys. Be sure the content and strategies are appropriate for your age group. For example, avoid software that requires reading skills if your class includes primarily 4-year-olds. Cooperative learning activities more readily foster team building, cooperation, and collaboration for partners using the computer than competitive exercises with scores and point totals.

Demonstrate several functions of the new software programs. Especially important are how to get started and how to quit. The software programs you choose to introduce initially should have consistent commands associated with the functions and features. This supports open exploration and independent use by even the least computer-experienced users.

Select software programs that consistently use the same keys or similar picture menus to access the functions or commands. Consistency across software programs also helps children become independent and self-confident in their computer use. If you work primarily with prereaders, be certain that the software supports speech capability. Instructions

*P*air children at the computer to enhance oral language development.

and feedback provided by the computer enhance children's capability to use the computer independently without adult assistance.

Time and Computers

Some classroom teachers use kitchen timers to regulate computer use and turn taking. They suggest that this method assures that all children have equal access to computers. However, we are very concerned about this strategy. Most early childhood teachers do not and would not limit children's participation in the block or art area with a timer. Imagine saying to a child engrossed in creating at the easel, "Sorry, Shanika, it is Jeremy's turn to paint. Your time is up."

After the initial introductory period, the computer center is no more a novelty than any of the other classroom learning centers are (MOBIUS, 1994). You can avoid competition for the computer center if you ensure that *every* classroom learning center or area offers intriguing and challenging activities. We support having the computer center open throughout the classroom day. Not only does this provide you cost benefits but children learn that computers are indeed a useful and helpful tool.

Computers placed in spaces other than the classroom pose different time issues. The computer's location and limited accessibility impose external time restraints on children as well as teachers. In these cases, teachers must make professional judgments about time to ensure quality and appropriate use of technology. Consider whether your program or school would support installing computers in your classroom so you could truly integrate computers with your curriculum.

Child-Initiated Activities

Child-initiated activity is as important with technology as with other early childhood materials; this concept has implications for management of the computer learning center and supporting gender equity.

Teachers should offer the computer learning center as one of the many optional activities available in the classroom. Many teachers include the computer as an activity option during "child choice time" or "work time." Other times of the day that computers are "open" tend to be when children are arriving and when they are departing.

Even after the initial novelty period, access to the computer seems to be problematic when there is only one computer available to twenty or more children. The children realize the scarcity of the resource limits their opportunities for a turn. Such a situation promotes frustration on the part of teachers and children. It often contributes to eliminating or curtailing some of the child-initiated aspects of computer use. Often the teacher's response to this situation is to assign children a specific day of the week for computer use or to set a timer for 5 minutes, which gives more children a chance but seriously limits a child's engagement with the computer. Instead, allow children open access to the computer center during all times when other learning centers are also available. Remember, your overall goal is to effectively engage children at the computer center in the same manner that you would at other quality centers.

For teachers new to computers it is often disconcerting to have children in class with more experience and a higher comfort level with technology than you have. Get over it! You do not have to know everything—not every command or function of every software program. Part of the fun and enjoyment of technology is the joy of exploring with children exactly what the computer can do and how the computer does it.

Random key presses and mouse clicks are part of the exploratory process. These happen fast as the child moves the mouse here and there across the screen and presses the button to see what happens next. It is often beneficial, and some educators would argue essential, to have the child explain (review) how he or she got the computer to perform a specific function.

Such verbalizations assist a child in becoming self-confident about using the computer. The child is in charge and can make the computer do what he or she decides. Opportunities to review processes and become involved in peer tutoring mitigate the randomness of trial-and-error exploration of technology. Exploration can be devoid of task conceptualization without the review of what the child did. The potential of a meaning-making outcome through trial-and-error exploration is not met. Computer exploration that persists in this fashion is disconnected from learning.

*P*eer tutoring promotes effective computer use.

The very nature of exploratory learning at the computer fosters collaboration and cooperation among the members of the learning community in your classroom. This learning community includes you as a learner, too. Relax and enjoy the experience!

CONSIDER THIS

As the teacher, support and advocate equitable access to computers for all groups (NAEYC, 1996). Researchers identify social class, race, and gender inequalities when children use computers for educational purposes (Sutton, 1991; Thouvenelle, Borunda, & McDowell, 1994). Apply the suggested strategies that follow to help ensure gender equity.

Equity

Observe children to determine whether girls have equal opportunities to access the computer. When boys outnumber girls in a class, sometimes the girls are reticent to approach and compete for access to the computer. Girls enjoy using the computer just as much as boys do, but they may not be as aggressive or competitive in vying for their turns. Clements (1998) suggests that if girls do not have access to computers before age 7, they're more likely *not* to be avid users later.

If girls don't have an equal chance to use the computer, you may have to temporarily impose a more structured schedule for computer use. For example, girls could have first choice for computers on Mondays and

Wednesdays with open choice the other days of the week. After girls have opportunities to learn and enjoy computer activities, they may be more adamant about getting their turns and competing with boys. But if they don't know the software and how engaging computers can be (because they lack experience), they may think, "Why bother"?

Some teachers, and even parents, erroneously interpret unwillingness to compete for computer time as girls' lack of interest in technology. "Well, girls just don't like computers as much as boys," they think. This is not so! Such misinterpretation can begin early and maintain pervasive negative effects that last a lifetime. Soon girls start acting like we think. They develop attitudes about technology, math, and science that we expect and are not really accurate.

Encourage all children to use and explore all learning centers in your classroom. You can make a difference by ensuring that girls get just as much of a chance to explore, experiment, and enjoy computers as boys do.

The type of software you choose can also affect girls' interest in using the computers. If you are predominantly using arcade games or competitive activities, these may not stimulate interest in girls. Look for software with intelligent female characters. Despite the number of competent women in the world, many software designers are stuck in a male-dominated, "superhero" mode. (Interestingly, male computer programmers outnumber female programmers three to one.) Be sure to select and introduce software that offers a variety of content and learning strategies that appeal to both girls and boys. See Chapter 2 on software selection for more details.

Other Locations for Computers

There are three possibilities for offering computers to young children: in a computer lab down the hall, as a mobile unit rolled into the classroom, or in the classroom itself. The ideal location that facilitates both teacher and children's use of technology is within the classroom, as we previously discussed. Teachers can more easily integrate computers into the early childhood curriculum when the computer center is part of the classroom environment. The lab option often disconnects children's classroom experiences from their use of computers because children must leave their classroom on a schedule to use the computers. The rolling cart is a limited blessing. Although the computer is used within the classroom, it is a temporary fixture and difficult to integrate with ongoing classroom activities. You may (or may not) have a choice regarding placement of computers. Here are factors to consider for placing and using computers in labs or on a rolling cart.

Computer Labs

Schools or community centers may install computer labs in their facilities for many reasons. A primary rationale is that the lab is a way to offer computer access to more children. A computer lab with twenty-five or thirty

*H*ave children work with partners to enhance learning, even in a computer lab situation.

workstations (computers) often serves an entire elementary school. Labs are definitely not the most effective way to use technology; however, due to funding constraints, they may be the only way to achieve any exposure at all to computers for your group of students.

Labs make it much more difficult to define and integrate the role of the computer in education. Computer use in the lab tends to disconnect the computer experience from other ongoing learning activities. The younger the children are, the more difficult it is for them to maintain learning connections across physically distinct locations.

Labs cannot effectively promote child-initiated use of computers. In order to ensure that all students in the school get their computer time, fairly rigorous schedules of lab time must be maintained. On the other hand, use of computer labs can help teachers new to technology begin incremental steps to full participation in use of technology. Teachers can, with the help of a lab assistant, begin gradually building their own comfort level without feeling threatened by having sole responsibility for the computers.

Although a computer lab may help the gradual introduction of technology to teachers and may support opportunities to scaffold teachers' learning about integrating technology with the curriculum, there is a downside. Lack of proximity to computers to the teacher makes the "bonding" process more difficult. Teachers must consciously set aside time to go down the hall to the lab to explore software. If computers were available in the classroom, the technology would be more readily accessible. With classroom placement of computers, teachers have them accessible for use during recess, rest time, and before and after school. They do not have to set aside a special time to go down the hall. Proximity equals convenience, and busy educators need as much encouragement as possible to make the time to learn to use technology. Keeping computers in the lab can mean "out of sight, out of mind."

Lab Tips.   Don't despair if you only have access to technology in a lab situation; it wasn't your choice or decision. Hands-on computer experiences in a lab may not foster the "best" experience for young children, but it can be better than no experience with computers at all. Here are some suggestions to enhance computer lab use for young children:

- Get involved! Find out what software is available in the lab; plan to spend some time learning to use it, or at least determine the nature and content of the programs, so you can respond to the children's excitement and the stories they bring back to your classroom.

- Make strong efforts to tie children's computer experiences with what happens in your classroom.

- Be sure to display in your classroom computer creations, stories, and computer art just as you do classroom work.

- Learn to use the available software and find out what children are using so you can respond in relevant ways to their learning.

- Be sure there are two chairs at each workstation in the lab, so children can enjoy cooperative experiences. This setup also stimulates rich language exchange.

- Accompany your class to the lab. If possible, stay and assist children who may need encouragement or help. With everything teachers have to do, it may be tempting to use this computer lab period as planning time, but your absence from the computer experiences of your children further disconnects the computer use from more traditional classroom learning. Your participation in your class's lab time enhances your opportunity to create meaningful links between their use of technology and classroom activities.

- Set aside time to debrief children when they return from the computer lab. Get them to review and summarize their experiences with the software.

- Get involved with the software selection process in your school or center. Identify content, educational objectives, topics, and strategies that offer meaningful learning opportunities for children, and then select software that matches these requirements. Don't waste children's time with software that is not suitable for their needs.

Computers on a Rolling Cart

Another limited option, the computer on a rolling cart, promotes computer use as a novelty experience since children have limited access for hands-on use. On particular days or times, someone wheels the computer into the classroom. The teacher also has limited access to the computer and is unable to plan adequately for its use. Perhaps the available time is short, so all children don't get a chance. Their time is up. The computer goes away until next week.

The rolling cart scenario is like having only one large, red fire truck that five classrooms must share on a once-a-week schedule. The novelty of the fire truck never wears off. Children are always clamoring to play with it because of limited time and access. Computers on mobile carts facilitate neither the teacher's nor the children's abilities to integrate the material (fire truck or computer) as a meaningful part of their daily experiences and routine.

Avoiding Common Mistakes

1. *Organizing the computer center to support only solitary computer use.*
   One of the areas where computers have the strongest impact is in the area of social development. Collaborative computer use greatly enhances the social learning of youngsters. Be certain your organization of the computer center supports this concept.

2. *Having the printers out of reach and unavailable for children to watch as their work prints out can be a problem.*
   Children end up taking risks (standing on tiptoes on a chair) in order to independently retrieve their printouts or to watch the printout being made. Watching the printer work is fascinating to many youngsters. We can help satisfy their curiosity safely by placing the printer in an easily viewed and accessible location.

3. *Treating computers as video arcade games.*
   Sometimes used as a reward (or even as a babysitter), these types of activities do not support using computers as tools. Although many software programs incorporate arcade and game techniques to motivate children to practice skills, it is essential for you to help tie their learning at the computer with an integrated curriculum approach.

4. *Supporting the notion through words or action, "After you're done with your work, you can use the computers."*
   This means you view the computer center as less valuable than other classroom activities. You do not understand or value the power of the computer as a learning tool. Avoid this by taking time to help children review their use of software and apply skills they practiced at the computer.

5. *Thinking that a printer is not an important component of the computer learning center.*
   Use printouts of children's work as you debrief about their computer experiences. Reviewing printouts can help refocus attention and encourage children to discuss and share strategies and

procedures they have used at the computer to create these print-outs. Articulating strategies helps link what often appear to be only trial-and-error processes at the computer with learning concepts and building skills.

6. *When selecting software, be particularly wary of products advertised as "edutainment."*

   Often these software programs are drill and practice wrapped in elaborate video and audio effects. Frequently the video and audio are irrelevant to the questionable educational content and concepts promoted as entertaining our children. Learning can be a very engaging, stimulating, and exciting experience. Appropriate computer experiences depend on wise choices that foster learning. Avoid wasting children's valuable time with frivolous and meaningless software programs.

7. *Believing that the computer center can be an independent learning center without any introduction or instruction.*

   Quality early childhood educators do not assume that children will intuitively and correctly use materials with unique characteristics. Even a common pair of scissors can be potentially confusing and dangerous without introduction. Avoid this common mistake. Teachers with limited computer experience are more likely to make this mistake.

Summary Points

- The preferred placement of the computer is in a learning center arrangement within the classroom. However, locating computers in a lab situation or on a rolling cart is workable.

- Ideally, each computer learning center has two computers and one printer (about one computer per ten children is an adequate ratio in early childhood education settings).

- Introduce computers and software to young children in the way you would any other new material or activity.

- Child-initiated activity is as important with technology as with other early childhood materials. This concept has implications for managing the computer learning center and supporting gender equity.

What's Next?

Now you know the best location for computers, how many computers you need, and how to ready them for operation as well as the importance of child-initiated activity. Next, you are probably wondering how to ensure your computer activities connect with your curriculum. The next chapter helps you do just that by examining your educational goals, connecting brain research with children's learning, and linking children's ongoing learning with other classroom activities.

Apply Your Learning

1. Use a large sheet of paper. Draw an outline of your classroom. Next, draw the location of these items:
   - Doors
   - Windows
   - Sink
   - Science center
   - Art center
   - Electrical outlets

   Choose the best location for your classroom computer center, using the chart (Figure 4.1) on p. 70.

2. Write a list of the equipment in your computer learning center. On a separate sheet of paper, design a space for each item.

   _____

   _____

   _____

3. Look carefully at the diagram you made in Activity 2. Do you see any potential problems? Write them in the following space. Consider how they might be solved.

   _____

   _____

   _____

   _____

   _____

   Make changes to your drawing in Activity 2. Look carefully again. Did you omit the problem areas (and avoid creating new ones)?

4. Write three basic rules below for children who use your computer learning center.

   a. _____

   b. _____

   c. _____

5. Write a lesson plan to introduce the computer to your students. Review this plan with another teacher who uses computers with young children. Make adjustments after you try it.

_____

_____

_____

_____

_____

_____

_____

_____

_____

_____

_____

_____

_____

_____

Linking Computers with Curriculum and Assessment

In the first four chapters, you learned about your important role as a central piece of the computer puzzle. You can also choose appropriate hardware that suits your needs, understand the importance of quality software, and set up a classroom computer center. Before we proceed with the critical connections between curriculum, assessment, and computers, we're obliged to briefly review essential software issues.

Quality software programs promote and foster links between your curriculum and assessment practices. The best software enables children to use the computer as a tool so that they experience and explore concepts rather than simply listen to someone talk about them. Offering children opportunities to control a microworld (a simulated environment) helps them become more inventive and better problem solvers. Good software meets children where they are and pushes their thinking further. Additionally, the best software supports cooperation and collaboration versus encouraging competition by keeping score or promoting winning at any "cost."

Comprehensive software that incorporates easy links with curriculum and assessment provides the foundation for your professional teaching activities. Such software enhances the ease with which you can support effective teaching and learning with technology in your classroom. Even if your curriculum and assessment systems are precisely aligned, when your software does not reflect appropriate educational principles, you'll have difficulty integrating technology. Careful selection of software can assist you in using technology as a foundation for your professional activities.

Teachers Ask

▶ *What do I do with computers in my classroom to support literacy, numeracy, and language development?*

Consult your national, state, or district-level curriculum standards for your grade level to identify educational goals for your classroom. Review your assessment and reporting requirements. Then use curriculum strategies such as learning webs, themes, or projects to create a meaningful framework that connects computer experiences with other hands-on classroom activities. Determine how computers can assist in the assessment process.

▶ *How do I foster collaboration and cooperation instead of competition at the computer center?*

Partner children at the computer and encourage turn taking and shared problem solving rather than competition and point accumulation. Include curriculum integration activities that incorporate cooperative learning strategies.

▶ *How can children with special needs benefit from computers educationally and developmentally?*

Computers can help us meet the challenges of special populations including children from diverse language backgrounds, children with differing abilities, and children "at risk" of educational failure. Computers support individualized instruction. Students with home languages other than English can hear directions and feedback in their own language. For at risk and special needs students we can modify and simplify activities and use special input devices.

▶ *What kind of computer experiences promote brain-based learning?*

Open-ended software that stimulates thinking about multiple solutions to problems also promotes the development of increased neural connections in the brain. When software poses questions that generate more than one "right" answer, it prompts thinking about solutions from different perspectives. This type of activity promotes brain-based learning.

After Reading This Chapter, You'll Know

- Organizational approaches and strategies that facilitate linking your curriculum with computer activities.
- Principles of authentic learning with linkages to software.
- How software supports documenting child assessment for accountability and reporting.
- Ways to use the computer as a tool for teachers and young learners.
- Brain-based learning strategies that stimulate the development of neural connections.

Reminder: The Teacher Is Key

We must reemphasize the fact that the teacher is key to effective classroom computer use. Acknowledging that the teacher is key to effective classroom computer use is the first step in analyzing the strategies that support achieving integration of classroom computers. A good indicator of successful integration is the extent to which general curriculum plans tie technology-related activities with literacy and other educational goals.

One of the grave misconceptions about computers is that you can rely exclusively on the technology to do the job of educating. You cannot ignore the human element (MOBIUS, 1994). Bowman and Beyer (1994) observe that, even in the age of technology, it is through relationships with others that children grasp meaning. Elkind and Whitehurst (2001) reminds us that computer proficiency does not necessarily mean cognitive development. Children will not become smart by learning how to operate the computer.

Samara and Clements (2001) echo this notion and emphasize the teacher's role to consistently mediate children's interactions with the computer. Teachers whose children benefit significantly from using computers are always active. They closely guide children's learning of basic tasks and encourage experimentation with open-ended problems. They are constantly encouraging, questioning, prompting, and demonstrating; this is the type of scaffolding that leads children to reflect on their own thinking behaviors.

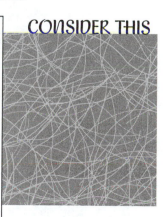

CONSIDER THIS

Appropriate technology is integrated into the regular learning environment and used as one of many options to support children's learning (NAEYC, 1996). A teacher's knowledge of child development, early education content, computers, and available software strengthens the relationship between curriculum and technology. Linking computer activities with hands-on experiences in other content areas fosters effective classroom computer use.

In the following narrative we focus on the ways technology can help teachers as they plan curriculum activities and focus on the nature of children's progress in gaining new concepts and skills. Each section offers a description of ways educators use technology to facilitate the teaching/learning process. These include:

- Providing access (via the Internet) to the latest curriculum standards from national, state, and district organizations.
- Connecting teachers with other educators to exchange ideas related to standards-based learning and accountability.
- Linking various curriculum approaches with classroom computers.
- Opening "a window to the child's mind" that provides teachers with a close look at a child's ongoing progress.
- Offering tools that permit children and teachers to reflect on processes and products.
- Adjusting computer-based learning activities to accommodate individual abilities and language requirements of learners.
- Supporting brain-based teaching and learning in the classroom.

National, State, and Local Curriculum Goals Tell Us Where to Begin

Increasing demands for more accountability in public education even at the preschool level have prompted national organizations to develop and promote standards-based learning for our youngest children. For example, the National Council of Teachers of Mathematics published *Principles and Standards for School Mathematics* (2000), which includes prekindergarten standards and outlines the mathematics that children should learn as they progress through school. This document provides a broad view of what mathematics is and can be for young children—a perspective that early childhood educators implementing developmentally appropriate practices can use. It identifies content and process standards (Richardson, 2000).

Closely tied to standards are issues of program accountability and measurement of the impact of educational services. In particular, an emphasis on child outcomes has emerged. Congress requires that all Head Start programs collect data three times a year on specific child outcomes and use this information to improve program quality. The Head Start Bureau recommends data collection in eight domains—approaches to learning, mathematics, science, language development, literacy, creative arts, social/emotional development, and health and physical development.

State legislatures are requiring similar program evaluation efforts. For example, California, Georgia, and Ohio, in a drive for program accountability, mandate data collection that documents how state-funded pre-schools make a difference in the school readiness of the children served.

Curriculum standards and accompanying accountability efforts are rapidly becoming a part of the landscape of public schooling at state and local district levels as well. States have turned their attention to the educational requirements of even their youngest learners. Arkansas, Connecticut, Maryland, Massachusetts, and Texas (to name a few) have published Prekindergarten Curriculum Guidelines. These documents inform preschool educators of what 3- and 4-year-olds should know and be able to do. Specific concepts and skills in subject matter and enrichment areas that are identified often include technology. Local school district alignment with these guidelines is not necessarily required; however, district compliance with state curriculum standards beyond kindergarten is generally mandatory.

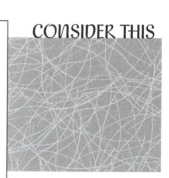

CONSIDER THIS

When used appropriately, technology can support and extend traditional materials in valuable ways (NAEYC, 1996). As states turn their attention to defining curriculum standards for even the youngest learners, technology becomes a tool that can enhance the teaching/learning process and impact children's cognitive and social abilities.

Using the Internet to Find the Latest Curriculum Standards from National, State, and District Organizations

Every federal government agency and national education organization has a website. Information on curriculum standards, accountability, and assessment are frequent and current key topics. Generally, the federal government agencies provide such information free of charge, whereas various national associations may require membership prior to accessing some content-specific information sources on their websites. Often websites provide helpful links to additional related information.

Almost every state department of education or public instruction sponsors a website that posts that state's curriculum standards and assessment requirements for schools. Frequently local school districts post their curriculum standards and accountability procedures on their own websites. Often schools create websites that summarize their alignment with district and state requirements and post results of standardized assessments. The recent trend is to publish documents (new and revised) in print and web versions almost simultaneously. Most of the time the version you access via the Internet will be more current than if you had to contact the agency and have someone there mail you the document.

Curricular Approaches That Offer a Framework for Instruction

As the wise woman once said, "There are many paths up the mountain." So are there many paths when planning and implementing curriculum. Each approach offers a unique perspective that identifies an organizational framework and strategies designed to achieve educational goals. Knowledgeable experts write entire books about just one particular curriculum or method of instruction. We offer you a brief summary of several "paths" to refresh your knowledge as you begin your trek. These include thematic frameworks, the project approach, and curriculum webs or emergent curriculum.

Thematic Frameworks

Using themes to organize instruction for young children has been popular since Dewey (1956) first proposed that curriculum should relate to real-life experiences. In developing a theme, teachers select topics they believe to be relevant and of interest to children and then build an array of lessons around that central idea. Such activities usually cut across the curriculum and take place either simultaneously or within a specified period of time. Relating activities through a common theme facilitates children's generalization of knowledge and skills from one experience to another (Eliason & Jenkins, 1986; Kostelnik et al., 1991; Machado, 1995).

Early childhood educators who use theme planning well incorporate into their teaching the principles of developmentally appropriate practice as defined by NAEYC. Such principles of practice form the foundation on which themes can be developed and implemented. Among these principles are:

- Providing hands-on experiences with real objects for children to examine and manipulate.
- Creating activities in which children use all their senses.
- Building activities around children's current interests.
- Helping children develop new knowledge and skills based on what they already know and can do.
- Providing activities and routines that address all aspects of development—cognitive, social, emotional, and physical.
- Accommodating children's needs for movement and physical activity, social interaction, independence, and positive self-esteem.
- Providing opportunities to use play to translate experience into understanding.
- Respecting the individual differences, cultural backgrounds, and home experiences that children bring with them to the classroom; and finding ways to involve members of children's families (Bredekamp & Copple, 1997).

Added to these optimal instructional strategies, theme teaching helps children develop an overall sense of direction and consolidation in their learning (Hendrick, 1986). Through theme-based teaching children build relationships among fragments of information in order to form increasingly abstract and complex concepts (Bredekamp & Rosegrant, 1992).

Concepts are the fundamental building blocks of ideas children form about objects and events in the world. They are the cognitive categories that allow people to group together perceptually distinct information, events, or items. As such, concepts form the bases of knowing, thinking, and reasoning. Children form concepts deductively through firsthand experiences. When they act upon objects or interact with others, children extract relevant pieces of meaning from each encounter. Through this cumulative process of experiencing, storing information, and testing knowledge, children build and modify their understandings of the world around them (Wellman, 1988).

Project Approach

The definition of the word *project* in the Project Approach has a very specific meaning: According to Katz and Chard (2000), a project is an in-depth investigation of a topic worth learning more about. The investigation is usually undertaken by a small group of children within a class, sometimes by a whole class, and occasionally by an individual child. The key feature of a project is that it is a research effort deliberately focused on finding answers to questions about a topic posed by the children, the teacher, or the teacher working with the children.

In the project approach Katz and Chard (2000) classify learning opportunities across three broad areas: (1) investigations, (2) constructions, and (3) dramatic play. Activities in these areas can require applying intellectual, physical, and social skills and concepts. Through these experiences children acquire new knowledge. The context for experiences leading to the development of new knowledge can be supplied by child-initiated or teacher-initiated topics.

The nature and types of questions that frame children's investigations are key to the Project Approach. Children make decisions about topics to explore and the types of learning activities in which to engage. They decide what to do, when and where to do it, and with whom to work.

The use of computers and software as tools to support investigations and constructions easily links with the Project Approach. Quality software for young children supports active strategies for exploring topics under investigation. Simulation software offers young children opportunities to employ "what-if" scenarios as they observe, record, and experiment.

Often constructions result from investigations children conduct. They integrate new learning by creating pictures, stories, or texts. Using the computer to develop such products permits children to reflect. The computer can also provide documentation of this process and offer teachers (and parents) a longitudinal record of the child's progress in acquiring new knowledge.

Microworlds enable children to employ dramatic play strategies as they take on the roles of family members or explore vocational choices by acting out the part of a community helper. In this way children integrate newly acquired information.

Curriculum Webs or Emergent Curriculum

Emergent curriculum is a planning process that takes place among a particular group of people. It requires that practitioners trust in the power of play and trust in spontaneous choice making among many possibilities (Jones & Nimmo, 1994). Many teachers respond to children's spontaneous questions and interests with curriculum webs that interconnect activities. In this approach to curriculum, a stimulus activity such as reading a book, for example *Mouse Paint,* may prompt questions about mice. Children may wonder about "where mice live, what they eat, what eats them, and what they do for fun." This can become the framework for considering a study of the topic of mice that extends to a field trip to the pet shop to purchase a mouse as a classroom pet.

Again, using computers and software as tools for exploring, investigating, creating, and constructing facilitates linking technology with curriculum.

*C*urriculum *webs help organize learning activities.*

Children use word processing to represent new knowledge.

Drawing and word processing programs can be used to represent children's new knowledge and understandings about the interconnections in the world.

Using Computers to Document Student Progress

One additional benefit of technology is that it can support documenting student progress in mastering concepts emphasized in the curriculum. Educators who carefully observe children using appropriate software can gain valuable information about a child's learning styles and thought processes. Weir and colleagues (1982) suggest the computer provides "a window to the child's mind." Software that provides a "window to the child's mind" helps educators examine student achievement in the context of meaningful activity. Look for software that offers features that permit children and teachers to reflect on processes and products created when using the computer as a tool.

Recording Ongoing Student Progress

Computers can provide educators with important tools that help document children's progress. When technology and assessment are well integrated, computers become an essential tool in the accountability equation. Computers can assist educators greatly when they are designed to support ongoing data collection, assessment, and reporting.

Authentic assessment is a cornerstone of evaluating children's progress. The computer learning environment offers educators and parents a window into the child's learning processes and development of understanding. We must take the opportunity to assess the child's interactions at the computer with peers as well as his or her own experiences with the software. The following are examples of the types of assessment that might be available in comprehensive curriculum-based instructional software. This type of software assists teachers in managing the instructional components of the software and student use of the computer learning center or system. Such software often provides reports that analyze children's work at the computer and may also offer the teacher or parent and family suggestions to strengthen children's concept acquisition and skills.

CONSIDER THIS

Used appropriately, technology can enhance children's cognitive and social abilities (NAEYC, 1996). With the increased use of classroom computers and the new emphasis on accountability in early education programs, there is every expectation that we will need to document technology's impact on child outcomes.

Summary of Individual Computer Use.   Summaries of an individual child's computer use identify the interests and preferences as well as the frequency and amount of time each software program is used. The summary lists specific skills and concepts practiced within each program. Reports to parents suggest at-home activities that will help their child generalize basic understandings of concepts covered in "favorite" (most frequently used) software programs. Teacher reports offer additional curriculum-specific activities that are designed to promote practice of skills and concepts through hands-on experiences. Through individualized tracking of computer use, task persistence in terms of a child's active engagement with each specific computer program is quantified.

Summary of Software Use.   This kind of report summarizes computer use across the entire class. The report includes a class summary of interest according to the software selections children have made. This interest inventory documents children's current subject matter motivation and assists the teacher in designing theme-related activities that are important to them. The teacher can rank order topics of interest to her class and respond with curriculum based on "emergent" interests of the class.

Story Analyzer.   Offering analysis of dictated stories and writing samples, this option evaluates word usage and sentence structure. Reports summarize the grade level of words that are used (either oral language vocabulary or written narrative). The printout offers teachers a quantitative analysis of a child's narrative oral storytelling (in the case of story dictation) or an analysis of a child's actual writing passage (when he or she uses the word processor). Stories (dictated and written) are archived and provide a longitudinal view of each child's progress during the course of a year.

Slide Show. This option permits a child to choose computer work to include in a portfolio to share publicly with teachers, parents, and peers. Documentation of a child's progress over time is provided through the work samples that are selected and described by the child. Through the portfolio process children are encouraged to invest effort in their products. Selecting products to include in the portfolio and deciding what to say about these give children some control over sharing what's important to them. The portfolio process offers children the opportunity of self-assessment and participation in the evaluation process.

These are examples of performance or outcome measures that managed software systems often provide. The software automatically collects and reports information based on student use. These data are collected unobtrusively while the child is using the software. Data are collected individually and a longitudinal record of each child's work at the computer is maintained. Viewing a child's work sample or portfolio only requires the teacher to access selected computer files.

CONSIDER THIS

Early childhood educators should promote equitable access to technology for all children and their families. Children with special needs should have increased access when this is helpful (NAEYC, 1996). Technology can help teachers individualize and make accommodation for differences in languages, learner abilities, and cognitive style.

Putting It All Together: How Classroom Activities Promote Curriculum and Assessment Goals

Begin with the curriculum standards for your grade level. Identify one specific area on which to focus—language arts, literacy, mathematics, or graphic and musical arts. The following example highlights how one of the child outcomes for prekindergarten or kindergarten in the Language Development domain might be approached. This example offers a technology-rich learning environment designed to enhance children's development of listening. Language Development might be approached from the perspective of creating a technology-rich learning environment that supports children's development of such competencies.

LANGUAGE DEVELOPMENT

Element: Listening and understanding

Indicator: Understands an increasingly complex and varied vocabulary

Identifying and naming colors are important building blocks of higher-level concepts. Color is a basic way objects can be identified, categorized, classified, and described. Classifying and sorting can require the recognition of similarities in color. Understanding the vocabulary required in identifying similarities and differences in colors is important for learning in both the domains of language development and mathematics.

To create a learning environment that promotes understanding and exploration of the vocabulary and concepts of color, use Electronic Easel (MOBIUS, 2000) or Kid Pix Deluxe (Broderbund, 2000) at the computer center. Paint mixing and drawing software support activities designed to help children achieve educational goals in Language Development, Literacy, and Graphic Arts. Some specific concepts include:

We see colors all around us.

We label colors by names.

We can mix colors to make other colors.

We can have favorite colors. We might not like some colors.

Listening and Understanding

Children practice receptive language skills by listening to and following the oral directions that explain how to use the software. All of the directions can be repeated by pressing the F2 key. Some teachers mark this key with a sticker. To repeat directions in the child's language, press F4 (if this language is available). Software features are summarized in a help menu (F1) that can be read aloud with the click of a mouse press.

Children quickly learn to follow multistep directions that permit them to use the paint-mixing features in Electronic Easel. Through a step-by-step simulation activity children identify and mix primary colors to create the secondary colors. They learn to identify and name colors. Once they mix colors, they can use these colors to draw a picture.

LITERACY

Early Writing

Take story dictation at the computer using the Amazing Writing Machine (Broderbund, 1995) or KIDWARE Writer (MOBIUS, 2001) while the child describes the picture he or she made in Electronic Easel. After you have typed in the story, have the child name the colors used in the picture. Print two copies of the picture and story. Keep one for the child's portfolio and let the child keep the other to share with family and friends.

These additional activities across domains offer opportunities for the child to generalize and master concepts, skills, and knowledge related to the required national, state, and district-level child outcomes.

Book Knowledge and Appreciation

Read the book *Color Dance* by Ann Jonas to a small group of children. Be sure to identify the title, author, and illustrator of this book. Point out that there are different shades of colors. Similar shades of color share the same label or color name. The colored scarves in this book represent the special colors used by professional graphic artists and printers.

MATHEMATICS

Have each child identify his or her favorite color. Graph favorite colors. Tally children's hair and eye colors, shoe colors, and so on. Record results on a graph.

SCIENCE

Provide eyedroppers, water mixed with food coloring, and large coffee filters. Let children enjoy watching colors blend on the filters. Dry filters and mount on colored construction paper. See what discoveries they can make. Encourage descriptions of what children observe. Record these as part of documenting the scientific process.

Smocks should be provided and the area well covered with plastic or newspaper to facilitate cleanup. Set any guidelines necessary for sharing and using food coloring.

SOCIAL AND EMOTIONAL DEVELOPMENT

Sensory Painting

In what colors would you paint a happy feeling? What color would you choose to paint embarrassment? Or sadness? Talk about these emotions with your students. Choose an emotion with them and let them decide the colors they think represent their feelings.

PHYSICAL HEALTH AND DEVELOPMENT

Fine Motor Skills

Conduct a hunt in the classroom for objects that are different colors. Decide how you will count and record the number of objects of each color that are found.

Gross Motor Skills

Use scarves similar to those in Color Dance; play creative music and have the children dance with swirling scarves. Point out how the overlapping scarves can create different colors.

The following example outlines how to integrate computers with curriculum and assessment activities suitable for grades 1 to 3.

PROJECT: DESIGNING A BIOSPHERE

Grades: 1 to 3

Curriculum Areas: Literacy, Science, and Technology

OBJECTIVES

Students learn to:

Explore the requirements of habitats suitable for the survival of most animals.

Use technology to construct a virtual animal, obtain information, solve problems, document findings, and publish results.

Use reading, math, science, and technology skills to design a biosphere that ensures survival of their virtual animal.

Collaborate in teams.

Share the results of their collaboration.

(continued)

PROJECT: DESIGNING A BIOSPHERE *(continued)*

MATERIALS

Provide assorted construction and art materials including some of the following: modeling clay, graph paper, popsicle sticks, toothpicks, construction paper, sand, cellophane grass, cotton balls, fabric scraps, cardboard, markers, poster paint, and so on. Use the following or similar software programs: Encarta Encyclopedia (Microsoft, 2000), Kid Pix Deluxe (Broderbund, 2001), Fun with Animals (MOBIUS, 2001), and KIDWARE Writer (MOBIUS, 2002) or another word processing software program, and suitable Internet sites about animals and their habitats.

OVERVIEW

Small groups of four or five students collaborate to construct a biosphere suitable for the survival of the virtual animal they have created. Once they identify the survival needs of their animal, they design an optimal environment (biosphere) that ensures their animal's survival. The biosphere is a balanced environment that promotes life, health, and survival of their species.

INTRODUCTORY ACTIVITIES

Each group uses Fun with Animals to combine the body parts of animals from different environments including the Arctic, African Savannah (Grassland), American Prairie Farmland, and the Sub-Saharan Desert. Once the virtual animal is designed, students examine the characteristics of the animal that make it able to live. They identify the kind of environment that would be hospitable to the survival of their animal.

LEARNING ACTIVITIES

Students consider their virtual animal an endangered species. They need to create a biosphere that saves their animal from extinction. Perhaps their animal includes part lion, part chicken, part walrus, and part Gila monster. Each team considers the characteristics and requirements for survival, food, shelter, and safety. They investigate the features of a biosphere that would ensure a healthy life for their animal. What food does the animal require? What are predators for their animal? What kind of environment is necessary for the animal to rest safely? How could an environment be adapted or a biosphere constructed to enable the animal to live? Students use a word processor to document the results of their team discussions, including a summary of requirements for the healthy living conditions of their endangered species and a list of investigative questions they need to answer before they begin construction of the biosphere.

Students use the Encarta Encyclopedia or appropriate websites to conduct their research and investigations. Based on this research, teams summarize their animal's requirements as the rationale for the biosphere they create. This summary becomes part of the information they provide in the final team presentation to the class. Teams use a variety of construction and art materials to create a biosphere. This biosphere is built to scale so that it accommodates the size of their virtual animal.

EVALUATION

Assess the rationale of the team for each element of the biosphere including food and water sources, safety, size, and so on. Review team notes for accuracy and conventional spelling and grammar. Work with students to design a rubric to evaluate the oral presentations. Have each team participate in an oral presentation of their investigative research and their resulting biosphere creation.

Using Computers to Individualize Learning Opportunities

The two most widely used operating systems, Mac and Windows, include extensive options to support access for individuals with disabilities. Video, audio, and other features can be adjusted to accommodate users with vision, hearing, or other physical disabilities. Many software publishers including Edmark, Intellitools, MOBIUS, and the Learning Company develop software to support students with special needs or other specific learning requirements. Chapter 3 offers discussions regarding technology adaptations for learners with special needs.

Supporting Access for Students with Special Needs

The nature of providing technology support for children with disabilities requires individualization. Many more severely disabled students need technology adaptations that are especially designed and programmed to enhance their functioning in activities of daily living as well as instruction. It is important to consult with professionals with experience in both special education and technology to ensure the match between technology and student best suits the individual learning and access requirements of that student.

CONSIDER THIS

Provide an environment that is developmentally and linguistically appropriate. Recognize that children have individual preferences, patterns of development, ability levels, strengths, ages, learning styles, and language backgrounds (NAEYC, 1996). Look for software with computer-based learning activities that accommodate the individual abilities and language requirements of young children (e.g., software from Broderbund, Edmark, and MOBIUS Corporation).

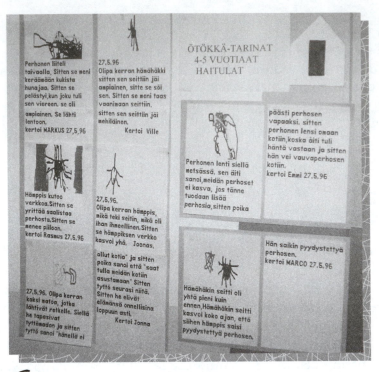

*S*ome software supports ESL Students.

Accommodations for Non-English-Speaking Learners

The capability of adjusting computer-based learning activities to accommodate individual abilities and language requirements of learners is sometimes a feature of the software. Broderbund, Edmark, MOBIUS, and the Learning Company are software publishers that produce software that can be adjusted to the language background of Spanish-speaking children. This capability not only enhances the learning experience for children with Spanish as their home language but also offers children who only speak English opportunities to explore and possibly acquire some fluency with Spanish. Some educators who genuinely believe that schools are preparing learners to meet challenges of a global society recognize the benefits of early second language instruction.

Brain-Based Research: Something to Think About!

Jensen (1998) and other researchers (Restak, 2001; Shore, 1997; Sprenger, 1999; Wolfe, 2001) maintain that the key to getting smarter is growing more synaptic connections between brain cells and not losing existing connections. It's the connections that allow us to solve problems and figure out things. Previously we thought the brain was hard-wired and didn't change. Binet, Weschler, and other early psychologists counted on that. They believed the IQ was fixed at birth and finite. According to them there was little that could be done to intervene or change the brain. However, recent discoveries have allowed us to document brain plasticity. Brain plasticity actually permits the brain to change based on exposure to complex environments. Today we know the brain continues to be available for changes even for adult learners.

The following discussion summarizes recent discoveries regarding the brain and explores the implications of these discoveries for us as educators. We consider how to apply this new knowledge to teaching and learning.

What We Know about the Brain

Three concepts are important in growing a better brain: (1) The learning is challenging with new information or experiences; (2) there is interactive feedback as a result of the experience; and (3) personal processing time is necessary to allow new neural connections to solidify. Challenging learning incorporates problem solving, critical thinking, relevant activities, and complex activities. Remember what is challenging for one student may not be for others; therefore, offer choices. The interactive feedback that is required should be multimodal, timely, and learner controlled. Since the brain is considered "social," take advantage of the availability of other learners to provide feedback. Journal writing and small group discussions give learners opportunities to reflect on new material and make associations with prior knowledge. These strategies promote linking new learning with existing brain structures.

Growing more neural connections and not losing any are the keys to helping children become smarter. To grow more neural connections, children need to take risks in learning. Providing a safe learning environment in which teachers encourage children to suggest more than one answer as a solution to a problem promotes this kind of risk taking. In such a classroom children learn to think creatively and suggest alternative answers or approaches. Helping children think about more than one answer to a problem or situation requires thoughtful teaching. Encouraging children to think and suggest multiple approaches promotes synaptic branching. This provides the potential for making multiple associations with prior knowledge.

So how can teachers foster the development of more neural connections? Brain-based learning activities stimulate thinking that enhances the development of neural connections between and among nerve cells. Asking questions of children is a more effective strategy for stimulating thinking than simply telling or directing children to think about an idea or concept.

Cardellichio and Field (1997) identify seven strategies that encourage neural branching. These strategies stimulate the types of thinking that creates more synapses between nerve cells. More of these neural connections help children get smarter.

1. Hypothetical thinking: What if . . . prompts children to engage in applying their knowledge to novel situations. "What if people lived in the zoo, and animals lived outside?" is an example.
2. Reversal of a known event: What if you were born before your brother or sister? How would your life be different?
3. Use another "intelligence" to promote understanding of a problem. Apply a different sense to the description of a problem or portray the solution in a different medium. For example, draw a picture to display a concept; write a description of a visual or graphic presentation; act out or dance your interpretation of an event or concept.
4. Analogy is another process that requires examining situations for similarities. This mental "stretching" encourages creative "out of the box" thinking.
5. Points of view imply taking another's perspective. A good example is the book by Gary Larson (1998), *There's a Hair in My Dirt.* This is the familiar *Goldilocks* story told from a worm's point of view. Point of view is another way to stimulate the development of neural connections as you try to maintain a consistent perspective of someone else's point of view throughout a simulated experience.
6. Completion requires thinking about a different ending or outcome to an event or story. One way to challenge thinking here is to have students rewrite the ending to a story or historical event.
7. Using web analysis includes trying to trace the origin of a thought from its beginning. Try to track a thought or concept from its origin. When did this first enter your consciousness? What made you think that particular thing?

How Can Software and Computer Use Reflect the Strategies that Enhance Brain Function?

Choice is one of the elements that is necessary. In a non-threatening environment children should be offered self-directed options. Negative consequences should not be the result of risks for thinking out of the box.

Computer software should be relevant and connected to the interests of the child outside the classroom. Tie curriculum activities to children's interests in order to provide a context for learning. Children can use the computer as a tool to express understanding.

Computer use should be collaborative and incorporate social elements. Partner children at the computer and use the computer as a tool to support project work. In addition to communication with peers, mentors and colleagues offer interactive feedback necessary for stimulating thinking. Be sure to include opportunities for children to reflect on computer activities. This provides critical time to make associations with prior experience and learning.

Summary Points

- The teacher has a key responsibility for ensuring that software selection supports his or her classroom curriculum and assessment practices.
- Technology supports many different approaches to curriculum.
- Appropriate software can promote opportunities for linking curriculum activities with assessment.
- Quality software that permits adjustments for students with differing abilities, languages, and learning styles supports effective practice for *all* children in the general education classroom.
- Software that stimulates more than one "right" answer and multiple approaches to solving a problem may enhance the development of neural connections in the brain. On the other hand, software that exclusively encourages only one answer may have the effect of pruning such neural connections and reducing the number of connections that support the thinking process.

What's Next?

Classroom computer use offers opportunities to enhance communication with parents and family members. Parents often express the same enthusiasm or skepticism for computer use with young children that early childhood educators do. Fostering open communication regarding these issues and exploring how technology can be used to provide more consistent communication with the home are topics in the upcoming chapter. Read on.

Apply Your Learning

1. Write your overall goals for math or literacy. Explain how technology could enhance the teaching/learning process in your classroom.

_____

_____

_____

_____

_____

_____

_____

_____

_____

_____

_____

_____

_____

_____

_____

2. List your current learning centers. For each center, choose software and integrated, hands-on activities.

Learning Center	Theme	Goal	Software	Hands-On Activity	Materials

3. Create an activity involving the computer that supports the development of neural branching. Hypothetical or "what if . . . " thinking requires thinking "out of the box." An example is "what if the capital of the United States was located in Kansas?" Such a challenge requires brainstorming the many possibilities that might occur if this were a reality. Try to create your own brain-based learning activity with the computer as a central ingredient of the task.

_____

_____

_____

_____

_____

_____

4. Contact your state department of education and request curriculum standards for literacy and technology. If you have Internet access, download this information from the website. Does your state include technology standards for prekindergarten and kindergarten that go beyond labeling the parts of a computer? If not, find a state that incorporates more of a "tool" use competency for young learners. Write up a technology curriculum standard and evaluation process that would ensure young students achieved the state goal.

_____

_____

_____

_____

_____

_____

_____

_____

_____

_____

_____

_____

_____

_____

_____

6 Involving Parents: the Home/School Connection

"About time," you might say. "Finally, some discussion about parents!" If you work with young children in no matter what type of setting, you interact in some manner with their parents. These exchanges may be formal or informal, pleasant or difficult, frequent or rare. Families can reflect diverse cultures, backgrounds, languages, and ethnicities. Each family may also have a unique composition of individuals who help raise the children in the household. In this chapter whenever we talk about "parents," we mean those adults who care about and are responsible for the children in the family. We recognize and appreciate that these adults could be biological parents, grandparents, significant others, foster par-

*P*arents enjoy using the classroom computer almost as much as the children do.

ents, or some other surrogate parent who is morally and legally responsible for ensuring a child's well-being. Our intention is clarity and inclusion rather than continually writing a comprehensive list of individuals. We hope that you agree. Just substitute someone's preferred title if they are in a nontraditional position but act as the child's parent, whenever you see the word *parent*.

Many early childhood programs and public schools are reevaluating their philosophy and practices regarding parent involvement. Although Head Start parents and program administrators make program decisions jointly and volunteer frequently in classrooms, such experiences are not common in other venues. Some teachers view parents solely as caregivers rather than educators. Others, with administrative support, are asking parents to become partners in children's learning and go beyond bringing birthday cupcakes or being the extra "pair of hands" on the field trip. A cooperative and collaborative partnership between parents and teachers benefits children as well as the greater community. These meaningful relationships support each child's growth and development. We believe this perspective is also true when considering classroom computers. With shared understanding of the appropriate use of computers, families and teachers can individualize children's learning opportunities and development. Additionally, learning about and using computers may enhance parents' skills and concepts. Continue reading and see what we mean.

Teachers Ask

▶ *How can computers support the home/school connection?*

Because parents are interested in computers and their children's use of technology, they are particularly responsive to receiving products their children have created using computers. Teachers send home activities and written materials that help parents understand how children learn. Such activities provide parents with examples of educationally appropriate activities targeted to their child's interests and developmental level. This increases parental participation in the educational process, whether or not parents are computer users themselves. Project samples, computer-generated reports of children's progress, activity ideas to use at home, and community resources are only a few techniques teachers can use.

▶ *How can children share what they do with computers?*

This answer is simple: Use the same strategies you use to share products developed with other materials. Send home copies of computer-generated artwork to post on the kitchen refrigerator. Start a continuous story or letter, written on the computer, and after writing a response, parents return it to school. If parents and the classroom computers have Internet access, transmit children's multimedia slideshows and stories via electronic mail. With this medium, you are limited only by your imagination.

▶ *Some families in my school do not have computers at home. Are there ways for them to learn how to use computers or access the Internet?*

It is amazing how many community centers offer free or low-cost access to computers and introductory computer courses. Classes often cover basic computer operation as well as advanced-level training on particular software programs. Although courses generally require a fee, computer and Internet use is often free once you obtain an identification card. The ease of locating public access to computers varies. Begin looking at the local library, public school, or community college. If these sites do not have public computers, personnel can generally refer you to some other agency or organization that does. Large communities (as well as military installations) often have "cyber-cafes" where anyone can use a computer for a fee. The modest cost is based on a specified amount of time. Organizations such as the Gates Foundation or companies such as IBM and Hewelett Packard contribute funding for purchasing computers for families and/or schools in some areas. Anyone who wishes to use a computer or have Internet access can generally do so.

After Reading This Chapter, You'll Know

- Methods to connect home and school with computers.
- Information parents need to know.
- Strategies for introducing parents to computers.

Using Computers to Connect Home and School

The days are waning when schools limit parent participation to baking treats, attending field trips, or participating in a variety of meaningless meetings. From all sectors, the parental role in education is increasingly considered a partnership with the school or center. The Bush Administration's White House Summit on Early Childhood Cognitive Development in 2001 emphasized building bridges between research, homes, and preschools so children may achieve school success ("Ready to Read," 2001). State-funded preschool programs mandate parent participation on curriculum advisory councils. Teacher education programs include courses on parent involvement techniques so that educators successfully include families in the educational process as well as computer methods strategies. Corporations such as IBM donate millions of dollars to schools for Reinventing Education technology-based projects. These projects are designed to foster better communication between parents, teachers, community members, and students.

Meanwhile, technology continues to increase in public schools and early childhood programs. Nine out of ten schools had Internet access in 1999; seven of those nine had access from one or more classrooms (Jerald & Orlofsky, 1999). Several have school web pages that include classroom newsletters, photographs of student work, Internet links for parents, and homework help pages. Many preschool and Head Start programs also have computers that teachers may use for instructional purposes (Bewick, 2000; Clements & Swaminathan, 1995). Computer availability does not appear to be an issue for many educators. (See Chapter 3, "Selecting Hardware," if you do not have a computer to use with children.) An ongoing challenge, however, is connecting this technology with experiences within children's homes.

Bridging Home and School

You say, "Enough already. Tell us what kinds of things we can do!" We hear you. Before we describe specific strategies, it is important that we repeat our position regarding parent involvement in education. (We realize that this may seem redundant to some but it is a critical point.) We believe that teachers are most effective in guiding children's learning when collaborating as partners with parents. Although some educators may perceive that they alone can help children's academic achievement, others recognize and appreciate the role parents play. Common sense tells us that children spend more time at home than in school. Yet parents often are uncertain what and how to promote learning for their children. Tradition suggests that many of us tend to teach as we were taught. These behaviors have varying actions and results. Our perspective is that teachers must help parents become more effective teachers of their children. This means using all available tools and materials to achieve this purpose. Children and the

Extend volunteer opportunities to other community experts.

broader community benefit when teachers team with parents. It all seems obvious. Technology, in particular, can act as the cement in building this cooperative foundation for learning. It serves as a tool that connects significant adults with young children's school success.

Reporting Children's Progress. Teachers can create a variety of child reports with computers, depending on the software program. Some programs automatically catalog lists that record the frequency and duration of programs children use, common activity themes, their achievement of educational skills, portfolio tracking, and specific home activities based on each child's current performance. These reports are easy for teachers because the software completes the necessary calculations and formats the final product. Other programs require that teachers input information and design the report's content and layout. If you have a choice, use the program that best fits your level of technological expertise and comfort with computers. The more you like "messing around" with what goes in the report and how it looks, and the more time you have, the more likely you'll be happier with a sophisticated program that allows a greater degree of manipulation and control. Computer Curriculum Corporation, MOBIUS, and Riverdeep offer these types of comprehensive software programs.

Some teachers use computer spreadsheets that indicate how each child is moving toward completion of specific child outcome goals. Other educators use computer-generated portfolio pages that include photographs and annotations of children's activities and projects. They assemble these pages into portfolios that illustrate children's progression through the program year. Teachers and parents review the portfolio jointly during scheduled conferences or home visits. Usually parents keep the completed portfolio at the end of the school year. We realize portfolios are not a unique method to record children's learning. Computers can make this process more manageable for teachers.

You can also send home copies of artwork, story dictation, early writing, number concepts, or individual assessments that children create with the computer in the same manner that you share other classroom creations. Pack up the materials, write an explanatory note or let the work speak for itself, give it to the child or directly to the parent, and presto, you've made a connection!

Another option (depending again on your software) allows children themselves to create documents and reports. These items respect the limited amount of time most teachers have and create a natural link between how a child interacts with computers and some sort of tangible result.

Sharing Classroom and Program Events. An important part of the home/school connection focuses on the broader context of the classroom and overall program. Parents want specific information about their children but many are also interested in other school events. You can develop and share a diverse and almost endless variety of parent-related materials with your computer. Help parents by distributing only what it is important for them to know. We have noticed that sometimes teachers send reams of documents to busy families rather than essential content. Think carefully about what you send to parents. By acknowledging and appreciating the unique concerns of your families, you increase the likelihood that they will read and apply these concepts.

We've included some suggestions in the following list. It includes many possibilities. After selecting one or perhaps two items, concentrate on essential points and important principles rather than everything that anyone knows about the topic. Remember, avoid sending home massive amounts of information. For example, our first item is curriculum goals and standards. We recommend that you choose one area of learning or a few standards. Write short but clear explanations about those selections, give a couple of examples, and then you're finished. We mean a maximum of one page of print, period. Parents will learn that you value not only their efforts but their time as well. As you read our list, check those items that you might consider.

- Curriculum goals or standards
- Child outcome indicators for your grade level
- Ongoing observation and assessment process
- Indicators of normal development
- Classroom lesson plans
- Extension activities parents can do at home
- Newsletters
- Upcoming and past field trips
- Contact and background information about community resource organizations

- Menus
- Employment opportunities
- Brochures about parent workshops and seminars

Anything on this list can also be posted on the program/school website, if one is available, by yourself or someone else. These items might be lengthier and more detailed than "sent home" documents because viewers of web materials make purposeful decisions about what and how much they want to read. (Parents receiving stacks of papers from school may throw them away; web users initiate searches for information.) If the thought of posting materials makes you fearful, give the materials to a more technology-competent colleague. Avoid increasing your stress level; many people enjoy doing this sort of activity, so allow them to help you.

Teaching Parents How Computers Can Be Appropriate at Home

As part of their professional responsibility, teachers must educate parents how computers can be appropriate with young children. Often this means that teachers must ensure that parents understand basic principles about how children learn. Seymour Papert (1996, p. 8) said it most clearly, "What parents most need to know about computers is not really about computers but about learning." This perspective is critical when teaching children between the ages of 3 and 8. As early problem solvers, they must engage in a variety of meaningful activities that employ three-dimensional materials rather than primarily paper-and-pencil tasks.

In Chapter 2, we discussed the importance of selecting quality software to ensure that this occurs. We also examined at length how teachers can appropriately integrate computers into the curriculum in Chapter 5. As an educator, you can apply these same guidelines when working with parents. Particular considerations also arise when working with parents. They include parental anxiety about school success, extreme attitudes toward children's computer use at home, and Internet concerns related to access and security.

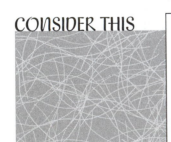

CONSIDER THIS

Collaboratively, teachers and parents should advocate for more appropriate technology applications (NAEYC, 1996). Teachers and parents must insist that publishers develop software programs using principles of learning applicable to young children. Both groups should only purchase products that follow these guidelines.

Parents and School Success.   All parents want their children to succeed in school, both academically and socially, regardless of their personal experiences with education. We contend that no parent wakes in the morning and says, "Today, I hope my child fights with other children" or "Hooray, Alicia is failing in science." Some schools struggle with effective methods of partnering with parents, especially for working parents or those families

*P*arents can play important roles in school and program activities.

confronted by several challenges. One way Head Start promotes the development of children's school readiness as well as the social competence of parents is by mandating agencies to design and implement family partnership agreements (DHHS, 1996, 1998). Many parents view technology as an important skill for being competent in today's society as demonstrated by their fund-raising for computer purchases or public relations for special bond issues to improve school technology (Ainsa, Murphy, Thouvenelle, & Wright, 1994). Children's education is the number one reason parents give for purchasing home computers. They report that family members use these computers mainly for educational purposes (Grunwald Associates, 2000, as cited in Revenaugh, 2000). Parents would not make this investment if they weren't interested in their children's achievement.

Our goal is helping parents view computers as positive supports for children's learning within a realistic and child-friendly context. Children can learn school skills and concepts with computers at home and school but they also learn in traditional ways. As we discuss in Chapter 7, the computer is not a magic solution for children's education. This myth-based perspective creates potential damage to children's curiosity and enthusiasm. Children reach their academic and social potential based on principles of appropriate curriculum and assessment when competent and technology-comfortable teachers complete the computer puzzle cooperatively with families.

Extreme Attitudes toward Children's Computer Use at Home. Each of us in the early childhood field must listen and evaluate concerns expressed by national organizations and leaders about parents, computers, and young children. The subject of lapware points out the wide range of opinions regarding children's computer use at home. Publishers distribute lapware, which is software designed intentionally for toddlers while seated in parents' laps. In fact, "Software manufacturers are tapping into the rich vein of parental anxiety. The fastest growing segment of the educational software market during the past four years is computer programs for children age 18 months to 3 years old" (Owens, 2001, p. C10). T. Berry Brazelton, a respected pediatrician, considers lapware an assault on children's minds. You've already read our position throughout this book. We firmly believe that children must be at least 3 years old before using computers, and then, within several connecting factors that ensure appropriate use.

Seymour Papert (1996), a researcher in computers and education, describes cybercritics and cybertopians. Papert says, "Cybertopians praise the wonders of the digital age. Cybercritics warn of dire dangers" (1996, p. 17). He views both positions as right and wrong. So do we, especially when looking at this issue from a parent perspective. When used for educational purposes at home, computers are neither all bad nor all good. Computers used at home create a variety of learning opportunities but parents can easily use them inappropriately as described in the lapware example. Drill and practice software provides close-ended experiences. Many parents would not tolerate this type of activity in program or school environments. On the other hand, parents who provide no opportunity for their children to experience technology place themselves at the other end of the scale. Acting as if computers do not exist in this society is a form of denial that holds few benefits for children. We promote a balanced and reasonable approach and, as professionals, ask you to help families to consider a similar perspective.

Parents and the Internet.   Parents who have Internet access worry about protecting their privacy and finding responsible resources for children and themselves. We devote Chapter 8 to the Internet since it is such a broad and important subject. Here we'll concentrate on discovering appropriate resources since that chapter deals with the privacy dilemma. Also, ask your local librarian for additional materials and information. Libraries are common public places for computer access and frequently distribute brochures related to parents and computers.

Various organizations have established websites and links to other locations with a family focus. Books such as this one are limited because of (1) the vast number of sites and (2) the frequency with which sites begin . . . and fail. Therefore, our suggestions are mostly broad rather than specific. Nothing is more frustrating than reading about a website and finding out that it no longer exists.

Begin looking at national and state departments of education. Use combinations of the keywords "families," "technology" (or "computers"), and "education" or similar keywords when searching their sites. Many will also refer you to other links. Also, check out the American Library Association's site at www.ala.org. It offers top ten Internet sites for families, technical tips, and even an online Internet introduction course. State and local libraries often have websites that connect parents to useful recommendations. The George Lucas Foundation at www.glef.org gathers and distributes innovative models of teaching and learning, using involved communities (meaning parents) as an essential premise. They also provide access to

*P*arents and teachers share concerns about Internet use with young children.

technology grants and programs that benefit teachers and parents. Government agencies such as the Federal Communication Commission have a vested interested in promoting accurate information for parents.

Look for other family-friendly institutions or organizations with websites at the local, state, and national levels. Use your search engine with the suggested keywords to find them. Always remember to consider the source when reading Internet ideas. You can generally trust the content if the source is credible.

Introducing Parents to Computers

Experts (Abilock, 1997; Haugland, 1997a) give examples of ideal parent/teacher collaboration. We consider education a successful partnership when parents engage purposely in school and home activities that support not only their children's learning but their own education as well. Computers can help significant adults in children's lives gain new skills and important information. These transactions can extend to the broader community through face-to-face and Internet contact with other adults and parent-friendly organizations. Although parents may not have computers at home, they often are interested in learning about them. Early childhood teachers may act as the catalyst for their computer education.

Classroom Volunteers

When early childhood programs locate computers in classrooms, they provide educational opportunities for parents as well as children. As one of many learning areas, parent volunteers can explore and experiment with

A parent volunteer learns computer skills along with her daughter.

technology as well as interact with curriculum and assessment concepts. An additional benefit applies to children. We have observed youngsters acting as teachers with timid parents. As they skillfully model mouse maneuvers and entrance into new software programs, parents who have not seen their children in this role before reconsider their perceptions.

Think about the parents of your students. How can you support their learning about computers when they volunteer? How can your children assist in this process? What types of materials can parents create with computers that support your curriculum? Avoid limiting your ideas; the possibilities are endless.

School Parent Night

You might also consider another option—the school parent night. After the school day, administrators and teachers organize computer education forums for parents. Facilitators introduce the Internet with multimedia sessions and give parents opportunities to manipulate the same programs that their children use during the day (Rosenberg, 1998). Computer-phobic adults are enticed to ask questions and experiment with unfamiliar technology systems with other individuals who have similar feelings.

Parent Computer Home Study Clubs are another variation. The school hosts monthly evening meetings for parents. They focus on new technological products as well as demonstrate and make available "shareware" programs evaluated for educational value. Demonstrations of new hardware, printers, and other equipment are also common (Debenham & Smith, 1994).

Communities best suited for these types of events are those where geography, weather, and parent work schedules do not present potential barriers to attendance. Knowing your families well and being aware of what works best for them are the critical factors.

Cable Show

Cable television productions are a unique method for introducing parents to computers if you have the necessary equipment, technical support, and human resources. Consider following the example of MacDonald (1984) who produced and developed several cable shows on early childhood topics, including computers. She notified families via notices sent home with children and catalogs of upcoming episodes. Although initially time-consuming to create and produce, this venue may suit your families' needs and interests.

Case Studies of Parent Involvement with Computers

It is helpful to know the types of experiences researchers have had with parent involvement and computers. Ainsa, Murphy, Thouvenelle, and Wright (1994) describe case studies in which parents and family members supported and learned about technology in early childhood programs. Each example also acts as a strategy for extending and introducing computers to parents. In one case study, both parents and grandparents attended computer open houses and training, participated as classroom volunteers, and created multigenerational connections between their primarily Spanish-speaking homes and the school. Some individuals also raised money for additional computers with local businesses and organizations.

In another case study, teen parents attended computer workshops and learned reading, writing, and math, as well as word processing and career exploration skills. These workshops focused on hands-on activities and adult learning principles. The parents also worked cooperatively with their children and developmentally appropriate software.

Finally, a university lab school sponsored a computer weekend for parent volunteers. The parents tried computer software at home with their children, observed their responses, and completed a checklist. Other community volunteers (senior citizens, high school students) participated so the experience extended into the larger community.

Think about the available resources in your program, school, and community. What elements of these case studies appeal to you and would interest the parents of your youngsters? How can you begin the implementation process? What do you need to do first? Jot your ideas in the margins of this book or on a scrap of paper and move forward.

CONSIDER THIS

Head Start agencies must provide opportunities for parents to enhance their understanding of the educational and developmental needs and activities of their children (DHHS, 1996, p. 135). Teachers work collaboratively with families to discover their attitudes and actions regarding using technology at home and in school.

Helping Parents Become Computer Competent

Frequent challenges confront those of us who face a computer screen daily. Whether we attempt something different with our word processing program or our Internet provider home page format changes, we continually learn solutions to new issues. Our frustration is rampant when we install a new software program or wrestle with an updated version. These same situations occur with parents. Computer competency is an evolving process regardless of our previous experiences. This continuous learning occurs as a result of the rapidly changing computer hardware and software industry. When working with parents, three major issues emerge related to computer competency: the digital divide, family literacy, and training. Each addresses a unique perspective for particular groups of individuals. Continue reading and see what we mean.

The Digital Divide

If you work with low-income, limited education, single-parent, or minority families, it is likely they do not have computers at home. The National Telecommunications and Information Administration (NTIA), an agency of the U.S. Department of Commerce, collects annual data about American household accessibility to telephones, computers, and the Internet (NTIA, 1998). Its 1999 report states:

> The "digital divide"—the divide between those with access to new technologies and those without—is now one of America's leading economic and civil rights issues. . . . Over all, we have found that the numbers of Americans connected to the nation's information infrastructure is soaring. Nevertheless, this year's report finds that a digital divide still exists, and in many cases, is actually widening over time. Minorities, low-income persons, the less educated, and children of single parent households, particularly when they reside in rural areas or central cities, are among the groups that lack access to information resources. (NTIA, p. xiii)

These differences are staggering. For example, a family with an annual income of $75,000 is four times more likely to have a home computer than a family with an income of $20,000 or less (NTIA, 2000). A low-income White child is three times more likely to have a computer at home than a comparable Black child and four times as likely as a Hispanic child (NTIA, 1998).

Various national foundations, corporations, and governmental agencies distribute computers to parents or community institutions in order to reduce this accessibility gap. In 1997, the Gates Library Foundation donated $200 million to U.S. libraries in low-income communities (Chapman & Rhodes, 1997). The Microsoft and Toshiba companies subsidize laptop purchases by students with their Learning with Laptops initiative (Romano, 1998). The Department of Housing and Urban Development (HUD) promotes Neighborhood Networks by establishing computerized learning centers in HUD insured and assisted housing developments (Beacham & Henry, 1997). Sometimes researchers give families free Internet access and computers donated by local organizations (McCollum, 1997).

*F*amily members support youngsters in gaining skills.

What does this mean to you as an early childhood educator? You may work in a community that receives technology support as described previously. If not, your community may meet certain donor eligibility requirements. Contact local technology, community, or governmental leaders for more information. Look also on the Internet for new technology initiatives. The digital divide exists and many resources are being applied to reduce this gap.

Family Literacy

Combining computers with family literacy programs enhances adult and child literacy skills. These efforts help parents teach literacy skills to their children while increasing their own educational and employment opportunities. Federal grant programs such as Even Start as well as nonprofit organizations such as the Barbara Bush Foundation support family literacy by educating the general public and funding various literacy projects. You can apply computers to family literacy initiatives in your own program even if you do not receive these kinds of funds.

Weinberger (1996) argues that access to home computers is a significant factor for children's literacy development yet parents also benefit by learning literacy concepts with computers. These benefits became clear during the 1987 pilot phase of Head Start/IBM Partnership Project (Ainsa, Murphy, Thouvenelle, & Wright, 1994). Although designed to examine children's use of classroom computers, researchers soon noticed how parents with limited literacy skills increased their competency by interacting with literacy-based software programs. Another Head Start program uses a similar process by connecting parents and teachers with a technology-based educational network (Hughes, Coyne, & Waddell, 1997). Computers are a strong component of a Chicago-based Even Start program that also uses photography and video technology to document progress of parents and their children (Landerholm, Karr, & Mushi, 2000). We are personally acquainted with several parents who because of their early childhood program became so technologically competent that they entered new career fields.

How you decide to use computers with your family literacy initiatives depends on the families you serve and available resources. You may choose to host "Early Reading" workshops if you work with a large number of limited literacy adults. These group sessions use computers to help parents learn how to assist their children at home and also increase adult skills. On the other hand, individual sessions might be more effective when only a few parents have difficulty with literacy and lack of experiences with computers. Remember to respect each adult's background and experiences, no matter what path you select.

Training

Training parents with computers takes a variety of forms. Most common are traditional computer classes where individuals learn basic operations and word processing skills, generally in computer labs. Many community education programs offer primary and advanced computer classes during the evening at schools when students are not present. Parents may also participate in distance learning courses for high school or postsecondary-degree completion.

Summary Points

- Teacher and parents must form cooperative partnerships to ensure quality use of home computers with young children.
- Children's computer projects and teacher-generated materials help bridge the gap between home and school.
- Educators can support parents by introducing computers and increasing their computer competency.

What's Next?

There are only two more chapters before you finish this book. We began by letting you know what an important piece of the computer puzzle you are. Next, you learned about selecting needed hardware and quality software so that you could implement appropriate computer experiences for young children. We also considered how computers could be integrated with your curriculum and assessment systems. Finally, in this chapter we presented supporting rationale and a variety of strategies for involving parents. When you read Chapter 7, you'll review common myths we hear frequently from teachers of young children. We challenge you to examine your belief system.

Apply Your Learning

1. Write three strategies for using your computer to report children's progress to their parents.

_____

_____

_____

_____

_____

_____

_____

_____

2. Describe methods to help your parents select quality software for home use.

_____

_____

_____

_____

_____

_____

_____

_____

3. Describe three ways that you can help parents use the Internet effectively.

_____

_____

_____

_____

_____

_____

_____

_____

4. Design a hands-on parent workshop to introduce computers. Decide what you want to accomplish as a result of this session. Write your agenda and the invitation you will send home.

A. *Parent workshop planning chart*

Workshop Objective		Personnel	Resources	Date	Evaluation

B. *Parent workshop agenda*
Draft your agenda below, using information from the Parent Workshop Planning Sheet.

_____

_____

_____

_____

_____

_____

_____

_____

_____

_____

_____

_____

_____

_____

_____

_____

_____

_____

_____

_____

_____

_____

_____

C. *Parent workshop invitation*
   Sketch your invitation in the space provided. Use your computer to
   write and print out these invitations.

5. Besides your program, where can parents use computers or connect
   to the Internet in your community? Write these locations and the
   related information in the following table.

Location	Phone Number	Hours	Fees

Confronting Common Myths

"Wait a minute. I glanced ahead and the 'Teachers Ask' section is missing. I read those great questions and short answers so I can think about what comes next. Where are they?" This chapter is unique. Several years ago, near the beginning of the technology revolution in education, Hannafin, Dalton, and Hooper (1987) identified some barriers and needs related to computer use in schools. They noted that although society in general had enthusiastically embraced technology, schools were somewhat resistant. They think that beliefs about computers have caused some of this lack of responsiveness and that some of these concerns are based in reality and others are not. We want to take this opportunity to explore the continuation of some of these beliefs or myths. We hear each myth frequently when we talk with early childhood educators throughout the country. Although almost ten years have passed since we first began working with teachers and computers, these myths persist. Sometimes the format changes slightly, but the basic premise remains the same.

Participants identify these concerns regardless of the composition of our audience or location in the United States. Therefore, rather than a single "Teachers Ask" section, the entire chapter addresses common and enduring myths. We believe you will find this a chance to confront your own concerns and beliefs about educational technology.

Think carefully as you read each myth. Do you consciously (or unconsciously) believe the myth's underlying assumptions? Are you willing to reconsider, and perhaps rethink, what you believe is "true"? Have you presumed particular statements were valid, when in fact, little evidence exists? Whether you are an enthusiast or a skeptic, some odd myth may be lurking in your mind. Sit back. Let yourself relax as you discover what you *think* is true and what composes the stuff of myths and legends.

After Reading This Chapter, You'll Know

- Common myths teachers believe about using computers.
- Alternative perspectives about each myth.
- Ways to think and act differently.

Myth 1: Computers Are a "Quick Fix" for All of Education's Ills

This myth suggests, regardless of costs (well, almost), computers are *the* answer. No matter what educational issue we face, computers are the ready answer to the problem. If test scores are low, or teachers need to individualize more, or we need to increase parent involvement, or the digital divide is expanding—getting computers is the answer! To a certain extent we, too, consider computers to be an answer. Otherwise we wouldn't have written this book.

We believe that teachers can effectively and appropriately use computers to help solve some of today's challenges in education. However, the notion that computers can solve any and all problems in education is simply shortsighted and unsubstantiated. We do think that just getting computers without thinking about how, when, where, and why you're going to use them is a big mistake.

Several conditions must be in place before effective use of computers can occur. The decisions you make and the actions you take determine not only the quality of children's interaction with computers but also how well you integrate technology within the curriculum. By connecting your program context and computer hardware and software with the needs of students, you connect critical pieces of the computer puzzle. As the teacher, you ensure that each of these conditions is favorable to learning.

*C*omputers will never replace classics, such as hands-on block construction.

Computers and their support systems cost money. This fact continues despite lowered hardware costs. If you have limited fiscal resources, classroom computers may not be your best choice to help young children academically. Additionally if you are unable to monitor other related computer issues, for example, software selection, the value of having a computer is limited.

Computers will not replace classroom classics. No child's interaction with a computer can produce the same result as actually constructing a tall block tower or pretending to be a firefighter, complete with hat, coat, and tall rubber boots. No sophisticated software program will replace finger painting with thick, cool paint as child-created designs evolve and eventually disappear. Traditional activities such as block construction, dramatic play, and easel painting became classics because children use these multisensory experiences in order to develop and practice beginning concepts and skills.

Computers are one of many tools young children use for learning. They are not and should not be the primary medium for intellectual and social engagement. This is one of the few points where we agree with critics of computers in early childhood classrooms (Alliance for Childhood, 2000). Young children learn by interacting with their peers and teachers in meaningful activities (Vygotsky, 1978). Using computers to please parents or administrators results in an expensive disaster that can discourage active learning by children, especially if teachers more frequently have the computers turned off rather than on (Peck & Dorricott, 1994). Our short response to this myth is: Before you adopt computers, be sure to consider the way computers will be used in the curriculum. Define your purposes and expectations for the technology ahead of time. And it almost goes without saying, for early childhood classrooms, buy basic and traditional classroom materials first if your budget is tight.

Myth 2A: Computers Are SO Simple and Easy to Use, a Monkey Can Operate Them

Myth 2B: You Must Be a Programmer or Have Taken Several Programming Courses before You Can Effectively Use a Computer with Children

Myth 2 is really two sides of the same coin, each representing an extreme position. Computers are either deceptively simple or terribly difficult. As with most things in life, neither position is accurate. Taking an extreme position at the opposite points of a continuum rarely reflects reality. This is true with these myths as well.

We notice that particular groups seem associated with each perspective. For example, software developers and hardware manufacturers tend to belong to the "deceptively simple" camp. Their advertisements and marketing personnel proclaim how easy computer use can be. Sometimes they promote children's instant and remarkable educational gains once you adopt their product. Buy what we're selling, they say, and your life effortlessly becomes magical and successful. Do you remember the old saying, "If it seems too good to be true, it probably is" (too good to be true)? Ask critical questions if someone tells you how their system is simple and effortless. Expect sales personnel to describe each preliminary step before you can operate the product. Avoid anyone who brushes you off, acts as if your request is too demanding, or is just too pushy. There is no need for the hard sell in today's marketplace. Our economy supports competition. Yet it is your role to become an educated consumer. Computer systems today are easier to operate and set up than earlier versions, but they still require a modest amount of information and skill. For example, when one of us purchased a new laptop computer, it took a few minutes before we could figure out how to insert the power adapter, despite the color-coding.

On the other hand, many computer systems do not require intensive and extensive training and experience. Although someone else may have organized the initial operation, most adults are capable of effectively using these computers with children. No computer wizard checks for satisfactory completion of technology coursework or other indicators of sophisticated engineering before you "test drive" any electronic item. If you are a reasonable adult who can function in today's world, you are capable of operating computers and integrating them into the early childhood curriculum. A technology specialist is helpful for support and troubleshooting if the system is sophisticated and involves several computers. It is reasonable to expect this type of support from the vendor.

▶ Myth 3: A Computer Is Fragile. I'm Afraid I'll Break It (or the Children Will) and Destroy the Software Programs That Are Installed

This myth has enduring staying power. We first heard it when we began working with teachers and we continue to hear it today. Inexperienced technology users most often repeat this myth. Their fear of destroying or damaging the computer is real, despite the remote possibility that this could happen. Technology components today are relatively sturdy. Unless you take drastic measures—pouring water through the air vents, hitting components with a large hammer, or dropping something more than a few inches—it is unlikely that you or the children can permanently demolish the computer system. Young children may, however, place small objects in the disk drives that you only discover later when things are not working properly. When we encountered a problem with the drive reading the diskette, we found small plastic people and play dough shoved into a floppy drive. After some minor cleaning, everything ran properly.

The other major fear about breaking the computer is related to losing files, the electronic directions that actually run software programs. It is quite difficult to intentionally lose or eliminate a computer program. If you happen to accidentally access the software feature designed to delete or remove a program or data, most systems display a warning note, asking if this is what you really intend to do. After you answer "no," things return to normal. As developers write new software programs, it seems to us that they have increased these built-in cautions. Besides, computers arrive with copies of software programs. You can reinstall these programs if you missed the cautions and deleted the software. Children are unlikely to get far enough into the internal operating systems to be able to delete programs. If they do, you simply reinstall the software.

A related issue is losing information because the electrical power surged, some odd, unexplained thing shut down your computer, or you thought you saved your document, but you didn't. Anyone who uses computers has had this experience. There you are, typing along, and the screen suddenly goes blank. You sit staring at the monitor hoping that your words will instantly reappear. Some software programs have built-in safeguards for these circumstances. They allow you to recover your document and continue writing. You restore power, and like magic, your document appears. Even so, we recommend that you frequently press the Save key when writing any document. This small action will increase your comfort level and protect your time.

Myth 4: Everyone Knows More about Computers Than I Do

Read the advertisements in the Sunday newspaper supplement or watch your favorite television program and it might appear that this statement is true. After engaging in conversation with your friends, family members, or coworkers, you could convince yourself that nearly everyone is a more competent computer user than you are. Whether the topic is a particular software program or new hardware gizmo, people seem knowledgeable about something you find a mystery. The facts are much different than this superficial view of technology users.

Although in 1998 nearly half of all households had computers, it is difficult to determine how people use them (National Telecommunications Information Administration, NTIA, 2000). Common sense dictates that Internet access does not ensure meaningful and purposeful use in the same manner that a library card does not ensure the reader selects classic literature, or even uses the library, for that matter.

From another perspective, researchers have developed scales that describe varying levels of computer use by educators and school systems. Teachers progress through beginning stages named "getting on the bandwagon," "entry," or "awareness" and may achieve "full implementation," "transformation," or "refinement." Only small numbers of teachers actually attain the "nirvana of computer use" at the highest levels (Cory, 1983; Coughlin & Lemke, 1999; Moersch, 1995). The reality is that some people are more competent than you are and some people are less competent. Avoid spending too much time on this concern. Your computer knowledge is a continuous process, progressing with each innovative product and service you learn about and practice using. You just need to keep learning and moving forward.

Myth 5: The Nerd Phenomenon Lives On

Face it. Many of us think that people who effectively use computers are geeks who would rather spend their time with a machine than with people. We picture individuals who wear out-of-style clothing, recite mathematical formulas, and act socially inept. These "nerds" seem to have the answers to any technological problem we experience. We place these "gifted" individuals on electronic pedestals because they can spew out detailed explanations as our computer changes page numbers or capitalizes lowercase letters without any stimulus from us. Their hands race across the keyboard, rapidly hitting 100 different keys when we ask them to demonstrate how to fix something. Meanwhile, you aren't certain (1) what they did and (2) if you could do it yourself. The truth, however, is better than any fiction we could create.

We are unable to locate any scientific evidence linking geek or nerd characteristics with being an effective user of computers or other technological tools. Thank goodness. We believe it would be politically incorrect to do this but also difficult to measure. We promise you will not turn into a nerd or geek as you increase your computer skills. (Even Dan Gookin, author of several computer books for "dummies," believes no one should take these tools too seriously.) Teachers who easily operate computers have more experience and practice than the rest of us and work in schools with computer resources and support (Becker, 1994). There is no magic. You will not turn into a nerd. Who knows, some people might find you even more charming as your computer competency grows.

Myth 6: After Training All Teachers Are Quite Comfortable with Computers

Yikes, this would be great if it were true. Common sense and practical experience suggest that most people do not automatically and intuitively learn how to do anything new even with the best workshop leaders and staff development trainers. Whether it is downhill skiing or gourmet cooking, individuals with more experience have greater skills than the newbie. After you begin learning something new, you become more competent and perhaps feel slightly more comfortable than when you started. As you gain more practice, you increase your competency and confidence, trying greater challenges. You strive to find the right balance that avoids frustration but keeps you interested, somewhat like Vygotsky's zone of proximal development (1978). At the same time, however, a new skier is unlikely to attempt an advanced black diamond trail.

Peer coaching and mentoring help teachers make progress in learning how to use computers effectively.

Computers are similar. Sheingold and Hadley (1990) suggest that it takes nearly five to seven years before teachers fully integrate computers into their classroom. Other experts disagree about the reasons for teachers' lack of effective computer use. Cuban (2000) argues that teachers find computers difficult for instructional use due to the demand of other curricular requirements. However, Becker (2000) disagrees, saying teacher use of computers is affected primarily by their lack of technical skills. The more teachers know about computers, Becker contends, the more they use them. If the experts cannot agree, what should we do?

We gathered information from a few more experts. "Great," we hear you say. Limited evidence is available about early childhood teachers and their instructional use of computers (Bewick, 2000; Bilton, 1996; Edyburn & Lartz, 1986; Fite, 1993; Landerholm, 1995; Haugland, 1997b; Wood, Willoughby, & Specht, 1998). The needs for more than "one-shot" training and ongoing support appear as a common theme.

Several things occur in schools and centers in terms of teacher education and computers. Teachers may receive little or no training. Teachers often do not have time to experiment with their computer, to "play" around, and test out their emerging skills. Sometimes the content of the training does not match what teachers need. For example, the training content is about a literacy software program yet teachers want to know specific steps for using the software with children.

All of this means as you become more competent with computers, you embark on a voyage of continuous learning. Gradually your skills increase. You learn more. You become more comfortable and competent with the technology. Simultaneously, manufacturers develop new technological tools and publishers distribute new software programs. Avoid thinking everything stays the same because it does not. For example, as we were writing this book, it took one of us nearly an hour to figure out how to put a different heading on odd- and even-numbered pages. It was pretty frustrating but finally, the lightbulb came on. We hope you're impressed.

Myth 7: All Software That Is Rated for Use with Young Children Has Quality Content

Both of us would be wealthy women if we received a nickel every time we heard this statement. (We wish this were true, but it isn't.) Some software publishers use expanded age ranges (e.g., a comment such as "good for children 3–10") to increase sales rather than to ensure that youngsters receive quality programs. Have you looked at the calorie content of "no-fat" cookies or candy? Do you believe that "one size fits all" when you buy clothing? What about 0 percent financing? You arrive at the furniture store or car dealer, only to find so many rules that unless it is the third Wednesday of the month, the constellations are in a particular order, and your mother's name is Beverly, you pay a much higher rate. Many diet and exercise businesses

*M*ost children enjoy using computers.

use a similar approach. Face it. All of us would be fit and thin if there was a magic pill, but no such pill exists.

We believe that printing a rating on a software package is just that, writing a few words to increase sales potential. There are some exceptions, but they are rare. We feel so strongly about this myth that we wrote Chapter 2, "Choosing Quality Software," so you can eliminate the "rating myth" from your brain. Look closely at the software program even if it appears rated by a well-respected source. Is the program just a computer version of a ditto sheet or coloring book? How does this software support tool use by young children? If children could do the same activities just as easily with paper and a pencil, and a computer version does not offer any additional challenges or features, then avoid spending your money.

Myth 8: It Doesn't Matter What or If They're Learning, Computers Are Good Because Children Have Fun Using Them

Children "like" all kinds of things—Halloween candy, junk food, staying up late, to name a few. Just because they like or enjoy an activity or item does not mean that it is good for them. The same is true of using computers. We really think that computers can and should be considered a valuable learning tool. Children can use technology to support the development of active problem solving, thinking, and communication. Technology can expand young children's horizons as they explore virtual worlds or communicate with youngsters around the globe.

Remember that selecting appropriate software is critical for supporting children's active learning. Before you purchase edutainment software, please examine the underlying educational content. Is it something important for young children, or is the experience something that just wastes children's valuable learning time? Ultimately you are the judge, and you have the responsibility to positively impact the learning of those you teach. There are no "software" police just as there are no "developmentally appropriate practice" police who will enforce the professional standards of quality in terms of materials and teaching.

Myth 9: As Long as Children Can Use Computers, They Learn Skills and Concepts Quickly

Who suggested this idea? The peculiar myth that children who engage with computers achieve academic nirvana independently and automatically is absolute nonsense. No research supports this perspective of learning for young children. It reminds us of college students who believe they can learn the contents of textbooks by carrying them around rather than reading them. If you persist with this belief, we have a piece of Florida swamp land to sell you.

*L*ink computer use with hands-on materials to ensure that children master concepts.

When children use computers, their experiences have the potential for great social-emotional development and intellectual achievement. Yet nothing is guaranteed. These results happen only with the guidance of a competent teacher who connects the teaching/learning process with each piece of the computer puzzle. Teachers who responsibly select quality software and integrate computers into their curriculum foster stimulating environments and future successful learning experiences for students.

One piece of equipment will not and cannot make the difference in a child's future. Learning is composed of a variety of interactions with materials, tools, peers, adults, and ideas. Having said this, we do not discount children who are intrigued with computers when other materials or activities do not capture their interest. For some individuals, computers can open the door to learning when other strategies have failed. Your role as the teacher is to help children learn in ways that fit their unique talents, individual abilities, and family background. Your skill in this process determines the quality of your professionalism.

Summary Points

- Most myths about computers, teachers, and young children are often broad generalizations that have no supporting evidence.
- Learning about computers is a continuous process.
- Teachers must integrate computers into their curriculum so children can use them appropriately.
- Teachers make important decisions about using computers that reflect their unique perspective.

What's Next?

During this chapter, you pondered particular myths some teachers have about using computers. We may have challenged your personal beliefs. Perhaps you reconsidered opinions from when you first encountered a computer, whether your experience was positive or negative. Use your readjusted attitudes as you move to the next chapter about the Internet. Talk about myths and legends! They appear frequently in this arena. Trust us. Soon you will learn how to access the Internet, decipher a website address, connect with professional Internet resources, and protect child users and your privacy.

Apply Your Learning

1. Write your major challenge about effectively using computers, in general, or with young children in particular, in the following space.

   _____

   _____

   _____

   _____

   _____

2. Write three strategies to resolve the preceding challenge. Be analytical and logical.

   a. _____

   _____

   b. _____

   _____

   c. _____

   _____

3. Choose one myth described in this chapter or a computer challenge faced by a colleague. Design and write three action steps to overcome any barriers for that person's computer use.

   a. _____

   _____

   b. _____

   _____

   c. _____

   _____

Exploring the Internet: What, Why, and How

For the past ten years there has been enormous hype about the fantastic nature of the Internet and the World Wide Web. Heralded as the medium that will help bring prosperity and education to third world nations, it has also been indicted as the destructive force responsible for divorce and the erosion of family values. Of course, the truth lies somewhere between these extremes.

Although Soloway et al. (2000) acknowledge that there is considerable debate over the value of the Internet in elementary education, naysayers only slow the inevitable process; the Internet is coming to each and every school and classroom. Therefore, in this chapter, we explore the positives and negatives of the Internet and how you determine the Internet's place in your educational environment.

CONSIDER THIS

NAEYC believes that in any given situation, a professional judgment by the teacher is required to determine if a specific use of technology is age appropriate, individually appropriate, and culturally appropriate (NAEYC, 1996). There are many ways educators can use the Internet to support their professional role in the classroom. To extend their learning, reflect on practice and participate with colleagues in a virtual community of learners.

Q & A Teachers Ask

▶ *How can the Internet help me in my classroom?*

There are many ways that educators can use the Internet to support their professional role. Direct access can offer staff development resources including online coursework from degree-granting institutions. Access to communication with colleagues via electronic mail or bulletin boards can go far in solving the age-old problem of isolation in the classroom. There are also software programs and resources that can be used by young children in addition to these professional resources. However, direct access to the Internet for our youngest learners must be carefully monitored and supervised. Only with your involvement can your students realize the educational benefits of this rich information source.

▶ *Is everything on the Internet accurate? How can I tell?*

With the huge amount of information available through the Internet it is extremely important to critically evaluate a website for authenticity, applicability, authorship, bias, and usability. Although the Internet and World Wide Web are filled with valuable and helpful information, they also contain unsupported theories and misinformation. Although misinformation and deception are not usually the objectives, the viewer's knowledge of the author's intent is important. It is your responsibility to evaluate the content and information of the websites you use with your class. Question the authorship, purpose, and bias of the information presented.

▶ *How do I find valuable resources for my class and me? Can I get free software?*

This is one of the greatest challenges posed by access to the Internet. New and experienced users find identifying, reviewing, and selecting information of educational value time consuming and frustrating. Search engines are one resource that can help. Be thoughtful about your purpose for accessing and using an Internet search. What type of information or content do you need? What strategy or skill do you want students to learn? Be clear about your objectives and focus on your specific educational need for Internet-based resources and use.

Free software is always a "draw" for teachers. We seem never to have adequate resources to purchase the educational materials we think we need. Yes, there is "free" software; however, chances are there will be contingencies on your acceptance of the offer. You may need to register with the website (and then receive unsolicited advertising in the future) or worse yet, your students, while using the site, may be bombarded with commercial advertising. It's your choice. How willing are you to accept what might be required in order to access "free" software?

▶ *Is it safe for children to use the Internet? How can I be sure they are protected from unsavory characters and content and that children's privacy is preserved?*

Museums, governments, and public and private nonprofit organizations are developing websites for children and youth. The availability of extensive media experiences targeted to this part of the population using the Internet has grown fast and furiously. Many of the resulting websites offer children wonderful opportunities to explore the world, connect with peers, family members, and teachers, and share products (including stories, artwork, and music) reflecting their own individuality and creativity.

In addition to these educational opportunities for communication and creativity, commercial uses of the Internet by toy companies and media conglomerates targeted to children and youth have also grown exponentially. Due to the interactive nature of such websites it is possible for sponsors of commercial products to effectively integrate their messages with content that actively engages young users. Their purposes are to develop brand awareness and brand loyalty early in the life of each potential consumer. Generally children are not media savvy enough to separate the message from the medium. They are often enticed to "sign up" for the featured products.

Protecting children from marketers and predators is one of the challenges of the Internet. Federal legislation has placed some limits on companies that target Internet advertising to young users. Additionally parents and teachers can use "blocking" software to prevent youngsters from accessing websites with inappropriate content.

After Reading This Chapter, You'll Know

- The basics of Internet access and use.
- Strategies for determining the accuracy and authenticity of information and websites available on the Internet.
- Internet resources and websites appropriate for early childhood educators and young learners.
- Guidelines for appropriate Internet use for your classroom school or center.

The Internet as a Resource for Educators

It's a revolution, and we all want to be a part of it, or at least we think we do. None of us wants to be left behind in the digital dust of the information superhighway. So how do we get onboard and make the trip worthwhile? First, let's look at the practical aspects of the Internet. As educators, we're inherently practical; we want resources and tools that we can use in the "here and now" of our classrooms. We expect the investment of our own learning time to have a big payoff, and the sooner, the better. So let's look at what the Internet can bring to you as an educator. Specifically, what can you do with the Internet to support you in your professional role as educator?

Teachers can use the Internet in a number of ways. The Internet grants educators access to:

- Communication with colleagues and peers, and children's parents/family members (e-mail)
- Online discussion groups (listservs, newsgroups)
- Professional development opportunities including distance learning
- National, state, and local curriculum standards
- Classroom resources and lesson plans
- Downloadable software and courseware
- Information on almost every topic imaginable
- Government, public, and in some cases private databases

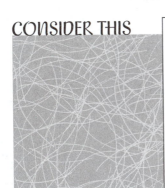

CONSIDER THIS

Early childhood educators should use technology as a tool for communication and collaboration among professionals as well as a tool for teaching children (NAEYC, 1996). Educators can use electronic mail on the Internet to communicate with colleagues, peers, and the parents and families of the children they teach. Listservs offer opportunities for active engagement with colleagues.

Educators report that e-mail and discussion groups are the most frequent way they use the Internet. These uses are not necessarily restricted to educational purposes. As teachers become more experienced with technology and identify effective uses for computers in their classrooms perhaps these two tools will be more widely employed in the service of education. As a matter of fact, a growing number of organizations are frequently incorporating these tools as effective ways to create and support a "community of learners" approach to their online course offerings.

Professional Development and Training

Two trends are driving the need for professional development: (1) technology in classrooms, schools, and centers; and (2) student accountability. First, educators need training in access, use, and integration of technology. Second, the focus on educational results includes not only documenting the effectiveness of technology use on student achievement but also teacher performance as it relates to accountability. In this context, we'll look at how the Internet can be used.

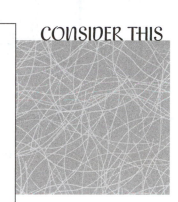

CONSIDER THIS

As early childhood educators become active participants in a technological world, they need in-depth training and ongoing support to be adequately prepared to make decisions about technology and to support its effective use in learning environments for children (NAEYC, 1996). Online courses offer educators an opportunity to gain basic practice in using the Internet and in learning how to link technology with classroom practice.

Distance learning provides educators an opportunity to respond to both trends. Online courses offer teachers ways to learn about, access, and integrate technology in the classroom. As a by-product of this effort, teacher computer use is often enhanced.

The availability of school computers with Internet access makes it possible for teachers to take advantage of anytime, anywhere professional development. Universities, colleges, educational organizations, professional associations, and commercial services are offering courses that simulate actual classroom experience without actually being in the classroom. Enrollment in some of these can be applied to degree credits or offer continuing education units. Others are designed to reinforce computer or Internet skills that may lead to certification in a specific technical area. Some educational institutions offer online degree programs. A good source for a listing of these opportunities is your state department of education. Generally your State Education Agency sponsors a website that promotes such offerings.

Despite major amounts of money, incentives, consequences, technical support, substitute time, hands-on computer workshops, and other resources for educators, the percentage of teachers using computers and the Internet for educationally sound purposes remains low. Clearly, professional development is crucial to technology integration. Online offerings can be effective and comparatively inexpensive. However, there still remains the issue of follow-through in the classroom. As we move from basic computer literacy skills, we need to focus on classroom use in meaningful ways. How do we ensure that instruction via an Internet-based course transfers into actual classroom practice?

Perhaps we need to envision a different approach to teaching when the teacher is teaching on a monitor. This shift could be toward inquiry-driven lessons with the teacher leading the learning instead of being the source of information. Some have referred to this paradigm shift in terms of the movement of the teacher from front and center to the sidelines—"the sage on the stage to the guide on the side."

We also need to move technology from being just a part of the system to being a *critical* part of the system. Focus on what we can do with technology that cannot be done as effectively with other media and materials. Before teachers can employ strategies learned in staff development computer workshops, they need to find them as effective and timesaving as their current strategies. Furthermore, teachers need tools to measure their own progress toward professional goals of effective technology use and integration.

Some sponsors of online staff development courses have found that teachers respond readily when online time is combined with the more traditional approach of "face" time. For example, online sessions include a group of participants and a site-based facilitator, who calls roll. This also provides teachers the interaction they need to learn technology through social construction of knowledge in a community of practice. Only when teachers participate in courses that reflect and model sound online learning can we expect their classroom practice to incorporate such strategies. Remember that teachers tend to teach as they're taught.

Teachers share the responsibility for effective use of technology with their administrators. Here are some areas that require organizational input and support. Key questions for administrators seeking evidence of measurable results from staff development initiatives include (Goral, 2001): (1) Can the school devote the time and resources to carry the new learning into the classroom? (2) Can the teacher successfully adapt it to his or her style? (3) Will follow-through resources be available? (4) Are curriculum changes necessary? Considering these issues optimizes the collaboration that promotes staff development experiences and ensures transfer into effective teaching practices.

CONSIDER THIS

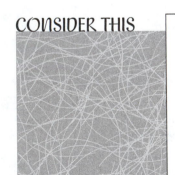

To achieve the potential benefits of technology, both preservice and inservice training must provide early childhood educators with opportunities for basic information and awareness (NAEYC, 1996). Within the domain of promising resources on the Internet it is important for teachers to become proficient in its basic use and to understand the issues and concerns that may arise from its access by children.

Basics for Effective Professional Use of the Internet

Admittedly there is a wealth of current information easily available for even the novice Internet user. It is important for you to understand the basics of Internet access and use, issues and concerns, and benefits and barriers, within this domain of promising resources.

To get online you'll need a few basics—a computer, a modem, an Internet Service Provider (ISP), some software to handle communications (Netscape or Internet Explorer), and a phone line. Once you've assembled all of the hardware and software and signed up with an Internet provider, you're ready to go. Now, you can send and receive electronic mail, join a listserv or discussion group, and explore the World Wide Web for education, information, and entertainment.

To facilitate your selection of hardware, software, and learning "the ropes" (or wires!) of Internet use, we recommend you have the help of a knowledgeable colleague or experienced friend. This person should be willing to be there when you connect the first time or two to ensure that you have the step-by-step protocol for access mastered. Although most Internet Service Providers have toll-free help, unless you have two phone lines, it is difficult to simultaneously follow their phone support directions while you're trying to access the Internet.

Once you get up and running, you'll want to engage in the most popular and widely used feature of the Internet—communicating via electronic mail! This feature, along with participation in discussion groups, and access to informational websites are the Internet resources that many educators view as essential to fulfilling their professional responsibilities.

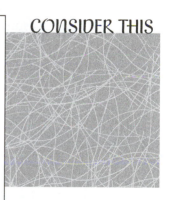

CONSIDER THIS

Early childhood educators should use technology as a tool for communication and collaboration among professionals as well as a tool for teaching children (NAEYC, 1996). The Internet offers educators opportunities to share ideas, strategies, information, and resources with colleagues around the world. In this way the Internet becomes a tool for teachers and helps them focus on supporting appropriate and meaningful learning with their students.

Internet-based discussion groups are extensions of electronic mail that promote sharing ideas and information around mutually engaging topics. Communication is possible regardless of the geographic location of participants. Exchanging views on educational topics, sharing information, supporting educational research, and locating classroom resources are often functions of listservs and discussion groups. Listservs and e-mail newsletters can be found on the Internet at www.liszt.com. Once you access a listserv with topics relevant to your particular interests, there are instructions for joining the discussion group. After subscribing to a listserv, you will want to introduce yourself to other members and identify your major interests within that particular topic.

Using Search Tools

The World Wide Web includes many resources that are linked together by computers around the world. These collections contain articles, lesson plans, photos from zoos and museums, documents, music, animations, videos, projects for children, and more—the list is almost endless. And that's where the challenge lies. You might wonder, "How can I find what I need within a reasonable amount of time?"

Well, we're glad you asked. Fortunately, there are Web search tools. These include directories/portals and search engines. Directories/portals are constructed with a hierarchical structure. They facilitate topic and category searching. They offer a good starting point for broad subject searches and tend to generate quality information rather than quantity. Suggestions for resources are websites rather than web pages.

Search engines use keywords or phrases to frame the information inquiry. There are numerous search engines and each has an idiosyncratic method for defining the search. You will need to follow the specific logic of the search engine you elect to use. You may need to define a phrase with quotes, plus or minus signs, or other strategies that narrow your search within the processing structure of that particular search engine. The results of most search engines generate a number of options related to the subject of interest for you to review and link to with the simple "click" of a mouse button.

Many search engines provide your list of "hits" with brief annotations or summaries of the article, material, or type of site that may contain additional relevant resources. Here are some of the most widely used search engines.

- www.askjeeves.com
- www.excite.com
- www.google.com
- www.ipl.org
- www.northernlight.com
- www.search.com
- www.yahoo.com

You may have noticed that there is a three-letter extension at the end of the name of the search engine. This designation often denotes the sponsorship of the material available at that site. For example, the fourth one on the preceding list has a three letter ending *.org* that stands for organization. Some additional common endings include *.gov* for government, *.edu* for educational, *.com* for commercial, and *.net* for Internet. These extensions should help you in determining the credibility and validity of information posted on various websites.

Your most important issue as a teacher is to maintain your focus on the primary objective of your search. Do you merely want to confirm that your curriculum standard matches or meets national, state, and local standards, or are you searching more broadly for options for assessment and accountability in general? Keep asking yourself, "What is it that I want to know?" Unless you keep your search objective in mind, you might find yourself clicking away in technology neverland without getting an answer.

General searches can be time-consuming and produce an overwhelming amount of material that may or may not fit your needs. Be very specific in the keyword or phrase you use to begin your search. If your search is too far from your initial intent, use one of the great features of the Internet. This is the "back" button near the top left corner of the screen. A simple click here usually returns you to a starting point that you'll recognize. This searching function does become easier with practice. Soon connecting with teachers and other educators to promote professional development and accessing idea and activity exchanges related to standards-based learning and accountability become almost automatic. You won't even have to think about how you did it!

Internet Cautions

Now we need to raise a couple of cautions related to the information you're accessing on websites. With the huge amount of information available on the Web, we want you to be able to critically evaluate what's accessible. Specifically, we want you to consider the accuracy and authenticity of what you're reading. Just because it is published on the Internet does not mean that it shouldn't be reviewed critically. Here are some suggestions for evaluating websites.

Authorship and Source.   What are the credentials of those providing the content? What organization, corporation, or individual sponsors the site? Is this a reputable source for such content? Is it a .gov, .edu, .com, or .org site? This should give you some indication of the purpose of the site.

Currency of Information.   When was the website introduced? How frequently is it updated? Do the links work? If not, then the sponsor has probably not recently updated this site. What is the schedule for updating the site?

Purpose.   The site's purpose often gives you a key to the bias and reliability of information. Why is this information being posted on the Web? What other sources either on the Web or published in more traditional format corroborate the information you've located? Is the purpose of the website advertising, informing, and/or soliciting? Is someone trying to market a product or a political point of view? Does the content reflect someone's personal philosophy? Is there a free offer attached in exchange for personal information? Is the site sending out "cookies" that permit the source to track your clicking through the content?

We raise these questions primarily to heighten your awareness of the need to be vigilant about how you are using the Internet. We recommend highly that you critically review and evaluate the content of the site and the information offered, especially prior to use in your classroom.

Professional Development Resources

Here are some websites that provide early childhood educators with professional development resources. A number of these include opportunities for distance learning. Remember each address should be preceded by http://.

- www.acf.dhhs.gov
  Administration for Children and Families—Information on Head Start and Child Welfare

- www.air.org
  American Institute of Research provides descriptions of projects and research in Early Childhood, Educational Technology, and Special Education

- www.aace.org
  Association for the Advancement of Computing in Education

- www.ascd.org
  Association for Supervision and Curriculum Development

- www.iste.org
  International Society for Technology in Education

- www.mff.org/edtech/
  Milken Family Foundation: Educational Technology

- www.naeyc.org
  National Association for the Education of Young Children

- www.nichd.nih.gov/about/crmc/cdb/p_learning.htm
  National Institute of Child Health and Human Development

- www.seca50.org
  Southern Early Childhood Association

- www.academypa.org
  State of Pennsylvania, Department of Education—Courses for credits or CEUs

- www.techandyoungchildren.org
  Technology and Young Children: NAEYC's Technology and Young Children Interest Forum

- www.ed.gov
  United States Department of Education

- www.ed.gov/technology
  United States Department of Education's Office of Educational Technology

- www.atl.ualberta.ca
  University of Alberta, Canada—Training in instructional design, Web, and multimedia production

- www.jhu.edu
  Center on School, Family, and Community Partnerships—An educational research and development center at Johns Hopkins University

- www.ala.org
  American Library Association

One more word about the Internet websites before we move on to children's access and use. Websites can be ephemeral. That is, they can be here today and gone the next day. These disappearances happen for a variety of reasons. Perhaps the sponsoring organization is no longer funded to provide the site, the server could be out of commission (then it's a temporary thing), there is a change in the host server, the links might not be functioning properly because of sunspots, you keyed in the website address inaccurately, and the possibilities go on. All you know is that you can no longer access the site. There are some strategies that minimize this inconvenience of "operator error" (you misspelled or miskeyed the address of the website).

When you find a site that you are particularly interested in accessing repeatedly, bookmark it, or mark it as one of your "favorites." This way the website is available for future access without your keying in the entire address. This avoids errors and lets you quickly access that site for updates. You can also easily print the information on the website of interest or store it in an electronic file format on your hard drive or floppy disk for future reference.

For a moment we need to consider intellectual property and the World Wide Web just so you won't be surprised and get into trouble because you inadvertently used someone's copyrighted material. Smedinghoff (1996), counsel to the Software Publishers Association, points out that a lot of people share the misunderstanding that if it's on the Internet it must be OK to take it. That is clearly not the case. Ease of accessing, duplicating, modifying, and distributing electronic files from the Internet doesn't make them any less susceptible to copyright and trademark law. So if you are creating your own web page, and you want to use images, sound, music, videos, and/or graphics available on the Internet, be sure that they are in the public domain or that you have permission from the copyright holder.

Creating Your Own Web Page

Talking about creating your own web page is not as daunting a project as you might think. The Hypertext Mark-Up Language (HTML), originally developed by physicists to support communication and collaboration among scientists, is not that easy to learn. Thanks to software publishers, today there are software tools that almost automatically "translate" easier-to-use web page programs into HTML code that is Internet ready. With these tools many educators can create their own web pages and help children learn to program and post their own web pages, too. This easy-to-use software has contributed to a proliferation of Internet web pages and has even been identified by some state education agencies as evidence of technological literacy.

Great, you say, that's all we need—more "stuff" on the World Wide Web—and who's reviewing what gets posted to the Internet? Good question. Many school districts have supported the notion that computer literacy includes students (generally, in middle school) creating their own web pages. Some state and local education agencies and public organizations have developed and posted guidelines for developing and submitting web pages to a publicly sponsored website. These published guidelines help educators (and students) review and evaluate the work before it is uploaded to the Internet. It is useful to find out whether your school or organization has any guidelines that outline policies, procedures, and evaluation criteria for establishing a web page on the Internet.

Here are some of the areas that may be covered in school district Internet publishing guidelines.

- Includes a clear educational purpose—the purpose could be related to an assignment or project.
- Protects the confidential nature of personal information, such as student names addresses, and phone numbers (including that this type of information requires signed parental consent).
- Includes photographs with identifiable information of students, homes, and so on only with prior signed parental consent.
- Links to other websites should be related to the purpose of the web page and should not contain any objectionable material.
- The content of the information on the web pages should not violate the privacy of others, be obscene or libelous, plagiarize the work of others, or include advertising for or material from commercial products.
- The text should be proofread, including captions, to ensure correct spelling, grammar, and punctuation.
- Copyrighted material including music, photos, images, videos, and written material should not be included without the express written permission of the copyright holder.

Information and Resources for Use with Young Children

Earlier, we made the point that perhaps effective technology use requires changes in our way of thinking about teaching and learning. We revisit that notion within the context of the discussion on using the Internet and its resources with young children.

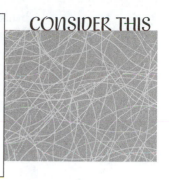

Appropriate technology is integrated into the regular learning environment and used as one of many options to support children's learning (NAEYC, 1996). The real poser of the Internet is how it uniquely supports learning. It can provide real-world experiences for young learners and foster collaboration and communication with children around the world.

The Internet and its resources offer lots of diverse content and reflect a rich knowledge base; however, just because students have access to this does not mean they will learn. The Internet is a wonderful medium for the exchange of information. Information availability does not equate to knowledge. We need to separate the hype of the delivery vehicle from its real power as a tool for learning.

The real power of the Internet is how it uniquely supports learning. It gives schools what they have been traditionally criticized for lacking. That is, it can provide access to real-world experiences and data for students in classrooms around the world. The promise of the Internet to center learning on the student instead of the classroom, to focus on the strengths and needs of individual learners, and to make lifelong learning a reality can be achieved most readily when teachers are thoughtful about its use. Improved access and delivery systems do not necessarily bring improved instruction. Improved instruction depends on the quality of the instruction and not on the medium through which it is delivered.

In addition to ready access to information, the acquisition of knowledge, or better yet the construction of knowledge, requires other very important activities. Practice with appropriate feedback, learner guidance, appropriate organization and design of instructional elements, inquiry into authentic questions generated from student experiences, and social construction of understanding through discussion are all required. We need to figure out how new technologies can be exploited in the service of meeting and extending these traditional requirements of learning. Only when we are able to apply these concepts and modify our curricula and practice will we truly achieve the promised benefits of technology. It is the professional responsibility of each and every one of us to try. Beyond information availability, another primary feature of the Internet can be used to foster children's social construction of knowledge. Once students have accessed information, they need to discuss what they have found within a shared context. Perhaps they share interests or pursuit of answers to specific questions. Such exchanges require communication in written or graphic format. Both offer ways for students to reflect on their own understanding of a topic.

The Internet can foster collaborative exchanges among students. Through these online interactions students actively engage in the learning process and construct their own knowledge. They generate new ideas and build on the thoughts of others. This helps clarify their own understandings of a topic and extend the opportunities to participate in a community of learners. Research has shown that students of all ability levels learn more when they are involved in such knowledge construction activities (Collins, Hawkins, & Carver, 1991).

CONSIDER THIS

> Teachers, in collaboration with parents, should advocate for more appropriate technology applications for all children (NAEYC, 1996). We need to work with all constituents (parents, teachers, policy makers, funders) to support the development of higher quality educational material for online access.

The Children and Technology Committee of the Association for Library Service to Children, a division of the American Library Association, in its 1999 online publication, the *Librarian's Guide to Cyberspace for Parents and Kids*, suggests these guidelines for selecting websites for children.

- Purpose and content easily determined
- Source and contact information readily available
- Content encourages active exploration and thinking
- Appropriate for the age and abilities of target audience
- Easily accessible with accurate and current content
- Features and capabilities exploit the technology of the Web

Some of the following are useful sites for students.

- www.vlib.org
- www.bigchalk.com
- www.britannica.com

 ## Issues and Concerns about Accessing the Internet

As we examine use of the Internet and World Wide Web for educational purposes a number of issues emerge. In December 2000 the Web-based Education Commission released its report, "The Power of the Internet for Learning: Moving from Promise to Practice." This report identifies barriers to using and developing the Web as a medium for learning. Barriers include (1) affordable access to broad-band communications; (2) better training for teachers and school administrators; (3) more high-quality online educational resources; (4) better protection and privacy for online learners; and (5) sustained funding at the school level to acquire and maintain new technology.

There are three areas where you as a classroom teacher can make a positive impact. First, you can take advantage of staff development opportunities that will help you use the Internet as a resource. You can gain the skills to effectively integrate the Internet into your curriculum. This will foster positive learning experiences for your students.

Second, you are responsible for the safety and security of the children in your classroom and school. This means you need to protect the privacy of children, so they won't indiscriminately and unknowingly provide personal information to commercial organizations. Finally, you need to protect children from inappropriate online content and predators. Fortunately there are software programs that can block objectionable content and there are federal laws designed to prevent the commercial exploitation of youngsters.

We advise against free commercial Internet filters because some feature advertising and others track sites that children visit and then sell this information to companies. There are many other options available.

The American Library Association (1999) developed some suggested rules for children accessing the Internet:

1. Ask permission before giving your name and any personal information anywhere on the Internet.
2. Tell someone you trust if you see something online that's scary or that you don't understand.
3. Don't respond to messages that make you feel uncomfortable or uneasy.
4. Never give out a credit card number or password online.
5. Never arrange to meet a person you've met online.

Even more important is teaching children to make wise choices rather than setting up external barriers and blockades against these commercial and exploitative practices. This is a challenge and requires sensitive and thoughtful discussions with children. Helping children become savvy users of technology, and in particular the Internet, gives them the skills to critically and to thoughtfully review the content they're accessing. We need to help children become critical and skeptical and willing to question Internet-based information and resources.

As educators we need to help youngsters become aware of the difference between commercials and what's real or factual. We can begin by helping them separate the accurate information from the commercial in the "infomercials" that bombard them on the Internet as well as on TV. Developing educated consumers of Internet content who can make wise decisions about websites to visit and personal information to share should be one of our primary goals of media literacy. When we are successful in this goal, we bring children personal freedom with responsibility, a lifelong attribute that is essential in today's technology-rich world.

Finally, we can join with parents and public policymakers and private and public organizations to support the development of higher-quality online materials and resources. Given our growing understanding of how children can learn most effectively with technology, we need to help translate this into practice. We need to collaborate with software publishers and sponsors of Internet-based materials to be sure that this new educational resource reflects the highest level of learning opportunity for our young children. In promoting access to the Internet we need to move from a "do not harm" mentality to one that actively pursues positive educational goals for student use of the Internet.

Summary Points

- The Internet can be a valuable resource for teachers and students. For teachers the Internet can offer opportunities for professional development, connecting with other educators, and reducing the isolation of the classroom.

- For students the Internet can be used as an instructional tool to support collaborative problem solving and co-construction of knowledge. Care must be taken to help youngsters avoid access to inappropriate content and the risk of unwittingly divulging personally identifiable information.

- The fabulous resources of the Internet can be used to effectively support teaching and learning when educators are experienced in technology use and understand that a new approach may be required to meet the potential benefits of technology.

What's Next

Well, congratulations! You've completed this book and you're ready for the next steps. We hope you've gained strategies and technical competence that make you comfortable and confident in using classroom computers.

We regard teachers and their organized expertise as central to our base of effective professional practice in using computers with young children. We urge you to try out what you've learned; to reflect on your successes and stresses; to share your effective and meaningful technology experiences with colleagues; and keep challenging yourself and your students.

We challenge you to contribute to the existing base of professional practice so others, both teachers and children, may benefit from your learning. There are many channels available that permit you to share your expertise. Here are just a few:

- Use the Internet and join a listserv that discusses issues related to computers and young children.
- Talk with colleagues about the software they use and what works for them in terms of curriculum and assessment.
- Become a mentor or peer tutor for a less technology-experienced colleague.
- Propose a workshop or submit a presentation on classroom computer use for a local or regional association for young children conference.

- Write up your experiences with classroom computers and submit an article for publication.
- Share your thoughts; send us e-mail at kidware@prodigy.net for Suzanne and bewickcy@pilot.msu.edu for Cindy.

Now that you have the skills and confidence to continue the journey, go for it! After all, learning is a lifelong process.

Apply Your Learning

1. Brainstorm practical uses of the Internet for your classroom. List several here.

   _____

   _____

   _____

2. List professional resources you think are available. Conduct a search. Document your results. Were they there? How easy was it to access and use the resources? Was the result of your search worth your time and trouble?

   _____

   _____

   _____

   _____

   _____

3. Write a set of instructions for a colleague about how to have a successful Internet experience. List your criteria for determining a successful Internet experience.

   _____

   _____

   _____

   _____

4. Here's an Internet quest that will challenge your search skills. Locate a website that is the source of information and can solve each challenge. Once you have located the website, carefully write down the address of the site. Compare your list of websites with a colleague's list.

   Find a list of the top 40 hits according to Billboard.

   www._____

Find three websites where you could get the cost of airfares from your closest airport to the Grand Cayman Islands.

www._____

www._____

www._____

Where is the closest theater that is showing a musical within the next month? Can you select a seat and purchase a ticket, too?

www._____

Who is Hollywood's top-rated box office star?

www._____

You missed your favorite show last night. Is there a site where you can find out what you missed?

www._____

You want further information on a news story you saw on the evening news. What website is likely to provide you with more in-depth details of the story?

www._____

You are interested in finding a new pet that's appropriate to your lifestyle. What website would be most helpful?

www._____

5. Access your state's web page. Locate the curriculum framework for the primary grades. Identify an area such as literacy, language development, or math and download the objectives. Create a lesson plan designed to use content from the Internet to meet your selected objectives.

6. Investigate what kind of software or filters can be used to protect children from accessing "inappropriate" material available on the Internet. Identify at least three different products. Analyze each in terms of pros and cons. Summarize your findings here.

_____

_____

_____

_____

_____

_____

_____

_____

7. Draft a policy for appropriate Internet access for students in your school or center. In addition to discussing access of inappropriate material, don't forget about the need for privacy and protection of confidential information. If your school does not have a current policy, perhaps this could serve as a beginning point.

_____

_____

_____

_____

_____

_____

_____

_____

_____

_____

References

Abilock, D. (1997). Parent Internet driving school: Using technology to increase parent involvement in schools. *Technology Connection, 4*(3), 12–13.

Ainsa, P. A., Murphy, D., Thouvenelle, S., & Wright, J. L. (1994). Family involvement: Family choices at home and school. In L. Wright & D. Shade, (Eds.). *Young children: Active learners in a technological age,* 31–50. Washington, DC: National Association for the Education of Young Children.

Alliance for Childhood. (2000). *Children and computers: A call for action.* [Online]. Available: www.alliancefor childhood.net/projects/computers_articles_call_for_action.htm.

American Library Association. (1999). The librarian's guide to cyberspace for parents and kids. [Online]. Available: www.ala.org.

Aquarium. (CD-ROM). (2002). Alexandria, VA: MOBIUS Corporation.

Barnett, W. S. (1995). Long-term effects of early childhood programs on cognitive and school outcomes. *The Future of Children, 5*(3), 25–50.

Beacham, A., & Henry, J. M. (1997). Neighborhood networks: Putting people to work. *Journal of Housing and Community Development, 54*(6), 31–35.

Becker, H. J. (1994). How exemplary computer-using teachers differ from other teachers: Implications for realizing the potential of computers in schools. *Journal of Research on Computing in Education, 26*(3), 291–321.

Becker, H. J. (2000, November). Is Larry Cubar right? *Education Policy Analysis Archives, 8*(15).

Bewick, C. J. (2000). The instructional use of computers by Michigan Head Start teachers. Unpublished doctoral dissertation, Michigan State University.

Bilton, H. (1996). The use of the computer in nursery schools and classes. *Early Child Development and Care, 125,* 67–72.

Binet, A., & Simon, T. (1916). *The development of intelligence in children.* Baltimore: Williams and Wilkins.

Bowman, B., & Beyer, E. R. (1994). Thoughts on technology and early childhood education. In J. L. Wright & D. Shade (Eds.), *Young children: Active learners in a technological age* (pp. 19–30). Washington, DC: National Association for the Education of Young Children.

Bredekamp, S., & Copple, C. (Eds.). (1997). *Developmentally appropriate practice in early childhood programs.* Rev. ed. Washington, DC: National Association for the Education of Young Children.

Bredekamp, S., & Rosegrant, T. (Eds.). (1992). *Reaching potentials: Appropriate curriculum and assessment for young children, Vol. 1.* Washington, DC: National Association for the Education of Young Children.

Bronfenbrenner, U. (1979). *The ecology of human development.* Cambridge, MA: Harvard University Press.

Buckleitner, W. (2000, May/June). "You haven't come a long way, baby!" at least when it comes to children's software. *Children's Software Revue, 8*(3), 4–5.

Cardellichio, T., & Field, W. (1997, March). Seven strategies that encourage neural branching. *Educational Leadership, 54*(6), 33–36.

Chapman, G., & Rhodes, L. (1997). Nurturing neighborhood nets. *MIT's Technology Review, 100*(7), 48–54.

Clements, D. H. (1994). The uniqueness of the computer as a learning tool: Insights from research and practice. In J. L. Wright & D. Shade (Eds.), *Young children: Active learners in a technological age,* (pp. 31–50). Washington, DC: National Association for the Education of Young Children.

Clements, D. H. (1998, February). Young children and technology. Paper prepared for the Forum on Early Childhood Science, Mathematics, and Technology Education, Washington, DC.

Clements, D. H., & Samara, J. (2002). The role of technology in early childhood learning. *Teaching Children Mathematics, 8,* 340–343.

Clements, D. H., & Swaminathan, S. (1995). Technology and school change: New lamps for old. *Childhood Education, 71*(5), 275–281.

Collins, A., Hawkins, J., & Carver, S. A. (1991). A cognitive apprenticeship program for disadvantaged students. In B. Means, C. Chelemer, & M. S. Knapp (Eds.), *Teaching advanced skills to at-risk students: Views from research and practice.* San Francisco: Jossey-Bass.

Cory, S. (1983). A 4-stage model of development for full implementation of computers for instruction in a school system. *The Computing Teacher, 4*(4), 11–16.

Coughlin, E. C., & Lemke, C. (1999). *Professional competency continuum: Professional skills for the digital age classroom.* Santa Monica, CA: Milken Exchange on Educational Technology.

Cuban, L. (1999, August 4). The technology puzzle. *Education Week, 18*(43), 68.

Cuban, L. (2000, January). *So much high-tech money invested, so little use and change in practice: How come?* Paper prepared for the Council of Chief State School Officers' Annual Technology Leadership Conference, Washington, DC.

Day, B., & Yarbrough, T. (1998). The state of early childhood programs in America: Challenges for the new millenium. In *Dialogue on Early Childhood Science, Mathematics, and Technology Education*, 29–39. Washington, DC: AAAS.

Debenham, J., & Smith, G. R. (1994, August). Computers, schools, and families: A radical vision for public education. *T.H.E. Journal, 22*(1), 58–62.

Dewey, J. (1956). *The child and curriculum: the school and society.* Chicago: Phoenix. (Original work published 1902)

Edyburn, D. L., & Lartz, M. N. (1986). The teacher's role in the use of computers in early childhood education. *Journal of the Division for Early Childhood, 10*(3), 255–263.

Eliason, C. F., & Jenkins, L. T. (1986). *A practical guide to early childhood curriculum.* Columbus, OH: Merrill.

Electronic Easel. (CD-ROM). Alexandria, VA: MOBIUS Corporation, 2000.

Elkind, D., & Whitehurst, G. J. (2001, Summer). Forum: Young Einsteins: Much too early, much too late. *Education Matters.* [Online]. www.edmatters.org.

Elkind, D. (1988, October). The miseducation of young children. *The Education Digest, 54,* 11–14.

Encarta Encyclopedia. (CD-ROM). (2000). Redmond, WA: Microsoft Corporation.

Fite, K. (1993, Spring/Summer). A report on computer use in early childhood education. *ED-TECH Review,* 18–23.

Fryer, B. (1999, November). A perfect fit. *Child Magazine,* 110.

Fun with Animals. (CD-ROM). (2001). Alexandria, VA: MOBIUS Corporation.

Goral, T. (2001). Professional development in a high-tech world. *Curriculum Administrator, 37*(2), 48–52.

Grandma and Me. (CD-ROM). (1995). Novato, CA: Broderbund Software.

Hall, G. E., & Loucks, S. F. (1977). A developmental model for determining whether the treatment is actually implemented. *American Educational Research Journal, 14*(3), 263–276.

Hannafin, M. H., Dalton, D. W., & Hooper, S. (1987, October). Computers in education: Ten myths and ten needs. *Educational Technology, 27,* 8–14.

Haugland, S. W. (1997a). Children's home computer use: An opportunity for parent/teacher collaboration. *Early Childhood Education Journal, 25*(2), 133–135.

Haugland, S. W. (1997b). How teachers use computers in early childhood classrooms. *Journal of Computing in Childhood Education, 8*(1), 3–14.

Haugland, S. W., & Shade, D. D. (1990). Early childhood computer software. *Journal of Computing in Childhood Education, 3*(1), 15–30.

Head Start Act, as amended. (1998). 42 USC 9801 et seq., 45 CFR 1301 et seq.

Healy, J. M. (2000). *Endangered minds.* New York: Simon and Schuster.

Hendrick, J. (1986). *Total learning: Curriculum for the young child.* Columbus, OH: Merrill.

Hohmann, C. (1994). Staff development practices for integrating technology in early childhood education programs. In J. L. Wright & D. Shade (Eds.), *Young children: Active learners in a technological age,* 93–104. Washington, DC: National Association for the Education of Young Children.

Hughes, B., Coyne, P., & Waddell, S. (1997, May). The technology in a Head Start parent center. Paper presented at the Annual Training Conference of the National Head Start Association. Boston, MA.

Jensen, E. (1998). *Teaching with the brain in mind.* Alexandria, VA: Association for Supervision and Curriculum Development.

Jerald, C. D., & Orlofsky, G. F. (1999, September 23). Raising the bar on school technology. *Education Week, 19*(4), 58–69.

Johnson, D. L., & Liu, L. (2000). Five steps toward a statistically generated information technology model. *Computers in the Schools, 16*(2), 3–12.

Jones, E., & Nimmo, J. (1994). *Emergent curriculum.* Washington, DC: National Association for the Education of Young Children.

Katz, L. G. (1972, October). Developmental stages of preschool teachers. *Elementary School Journal, 73*(1), 50–54.

Katz, L. G. (1995). *Talks with teachers of young children: A collection.* Stamford, CT: Ablex.

Katz, L. G., & Chard, S. C. (1989). Engaging children's minds: The project approach (1st ed.). Norwood, NJ: Ablex.

Katz, L. G., & Chard, S. C. (2000). *Engaging children's minds: The project approach* (2nd ed.). Stamford, CT: Ablex.

Kid Pix Deluxe. (CD-ROM). (2001). Novato, CA: Broderbund Software.

KIDWARE Writer. (CD-ROM). (2002). Alexandria, VA: MOBIUS Corporation.

Kostelnik, M. J. (Ed.), Howe, D., Payne, K., Rohde, B., Spaulding, G., Stein, L., & Whitbeck, D. (1991). *Teaching young children with themes.* Glenview, IL: Good Year Books.

Landerholm, E. (1995). Early childhood teachers' computer attitudes, knowledge, and practices. *Early Child Development and Care, 109,* 43–60.

Landerholm, E., Karr, J. A., & Mushi, S. (2000, June). A collaborative approach to family literacy evaluation strategies. *Early Child Development and Care, 162,* 65–79.

Lemke, C., & Coughlin, E. C. (1998). *Technology in American schools: 7 dimensions for gauging progress: A policymaker's guide.* Santa Monica, CA: Milken Exchange on Educational Technology.

Lerner, R. (1984). *On the nature of human plasticity.* New York: Cambridge University Press.

Lerner, R. (1986). *Concepts and theories of human development* (2nd ed.). New York: Random House.

MacDonald, J. C. (1984). Development and implementation of a television series for parent education on early childhood youngsters (Practicum report). Nova University, ED 251 238.

Machado, J. (1995). *Early childhood experiences in language arts: Emerging literacy.* Albany, NY: Delmar.

McCollum, K. (1997). U. of Illinois project gives poor people computers and studies how they use them. *The Chronicle of Higher Education, 44*(16), A30.

McGee, P. (2000). Persistence and motivation: A new teacher's path to technology infusion. *Computers in the Schools, 16*(3/4), 197–211.

MOBIUS Corporation. (1990). *Computers in Head Start classrooms: Recommendations from the Head Start/IBM partnership project.* Alexandria, VA: Author.

MOBIUS Corporation. (1994). *Computers in Head Start classrooms: Recommendations from the Head Start/IBM partnership project* (2nd ed.). Alexandria, VA: Author.

Moersch, C. (1995). Levels of Technology Implementation (LoTi): A framework for measuring classroom technology use. *Learning and Leading with Technology, 23*(3), 40–42.

National Association for the Education of Young Children. (1996). NAEYC Position statement: Technology and young children—ages three through eight. *Young Children, 51*(6), 11–16.

National Council of Teachers of Mathematics (NCTM). (2000). *Principles and standards for School Mathematics.* Reston, VA: Author.

National Telecommunications and Information Administration (NTIA), U.S. Department of Commerce. (1998). *Falling through the Net II: New data on the digital divide.* Washington, DC: Author.

National Telecommunications and Information Administration (NTIA), U.S. Department of Commerce. (1999). *Falling through the Net: Defining the digital divide.* Washington, DC: Author.

National Telecommunications and Information Administration (NTIA), U.S. Department of Commerce. (2000). *Falling through the Net: Toward digital inclusion.* Washington, DC: Author.

Neighborhoods (Farm, City, Village, Island). (CD-ROM). (2002). Alexandria, VA: MOBIUS Corporation.

Newmann, F. M., & Wehlage, G. G. (1993). Five standards of authentic instruction. *Educational Leadership, 50*(7), 1–9.

Oregon Trail. (CD-ROM). (1996). Duluth, MN: Minnesota Educational Computing Corporation.

Owens, D. E. (2001, July 26). Pros and cons of computer kids. *The Washington Post,* p. C10.

Papert, S. (1980). *Mindstorms: Children, computers, and powerful ideas.* New York: Basic.

Papert, S. (1996). *The connected family: Bridging the digital generation gap.* Atlanta, GA: Longstreet.

Peck, K. L., & Dorricott, D. (1994). Why use technology? *Educational Leadership, 51*(7), 11–14.

"Ready to Read, Ready to Learn": White House Summit Highlights New Research on Early Childhood Learning. (2001, September). *U.S. Department of Education Community Update, 91,* 1–3.

Revenaugh, M. (2000, October). Toward a 24/7 learning community. *Educational Leadership, 58*(2), 25–28.

Restak, R. (2001). The secret life of the brain. Washington, DC: Dana Press and Joseph Henry Press.

Richardson, K. (2000, October). Mathematics standards for pre-kindergarten through grade 2. *ERIC Digest.* EPO-PS-00–11.

Riel, M., & Becker, H. (2000, May). *The beliefs, practices, and computer use of teacher leaders.* Paper presented at the American Educational Research Association, New Orleans, LA.

Rogers, E. M. (1995). *Diffusion of innovations* (4th ed.). New York: Free Press.

Romano, M. (1998, February 26). With liberty and laptops for all? *New York Times,* p. G14.

Rosenberg, M. (1998, March 1). Parents test skills on school computers. *New York Times,* p. C9.

Sarama, J., & Clements, D. H. (2001, April). Computers in early childhood mathematics. Paper presented at annual American Education Research Association, Seattle, WA.

Schweinhart, L. J., Barnes, H. V., & Weikart, D. P. (1993). *Significant benefits: The High/Scope Perry Preschool Study through age 27.* Ypsilanti, MI: High/Scope Press.

Sheingold, K., & Hadley, M. (1990). *Accomplished teachers: Integrating computers into classroom practice.* New York: Bank Street College of Education.

Shore, R. (1997). *Rethinking the brain: New insights into early development.* New York: Families and Work Institute.

Smedinghoff, T. (1996). *Online Law: The SPA'S legal guide to doing business on the Internet.* Boston: Addison Wesley.

Sprenger, M. (1999). *Learning and memory: The brain in action.* Alexandria, VA: Association for Supervision and Curriculum Development.

Soloway, E., Norris, C., Blumenfeld, P., Fishman, B., Krajcik, J., & Marx, R. (2000, January). K–12 and the Internet. *Communications of the ACM, 43*(1), 19–23.

Sutton, R. E. (1991). Equity and computers in the schools: A decade of research. *Review of Educational Research, 61*(4), 475–503.

Taylor, H. H. (2000). Technology: A key to the future. *Head Start Bulletin, 66,* 1.

The Amazing Writing Machine. (CD-ROM). (1995). Novato, CA: Broderbund Software.

Thouvenelle, S., Borunda, M., & McDowell, C. (1994). Replicating inequities: Are we doing it again? In J. L. Wright & D. Shade (Eds.). *Young children: Active learners in a technological age* (pp. 151–166). Washington, DC: National Association for the Education of Young Children.

Turkle, S. (1984). *The second self: Computers and the human spirit.* New York: Simon and Schuster.

U.S. Department of Health and Human Services (DHHS), Administration for Children and Families, Administration on Children, Youth, and Families, Head Start Bureau. (1996). *Head Start Program Performance Standards and other regulations. 45 CFR Parts*

1301, 1302, 1303, 1304 and guidance, 1305, 1306, and 1308 and guidance. Washington, DC: Author.

U.S. Department of Health and Human Services (DHHS), Administration for Children and Families, Administration on Children, Youth and Families, Head Start Bureau. (1998). *Head Start Program Performance Standards and other regulations. 45 CFR Parts 1301, 1302, 1303, 1304 and guidance, 1305, 1306, and 1308 and guidance.* Washington, DC: Author.

Vygotsky, L. S. (1978). *Mind in society: The development of higher psychological processes* (M. Cole, B. John-Steiner, S. Scribner, & E. Souberman, Eds. and Trans.). Cambridge, MA: Harvard University Press.

Web-Based Education Commission. (2000). *The power of the Internet for learning: Moving from promise to practice.* [Online]. Available: www.webcommission.org.

Weinberger, J. (1996). A longitudinal study of children's early literacy experiences at home and later literacy development at home and school. *Journal of Research in Reading* (19), 14–24.

Weir, S., Russell, S. J., & Valente, J. A. (1982). Logo: An approach to educating disabled children. *BYTE, 1*(8): 342–360.

Wellman, H. M. (1988). First steps in the child's theorizing about the mind. In J. Astington, P. L. Harris, & D. R. Olson (Eds.), *Developing theories of mind.* New York: Cambridge University Press.

Wenglinsky, H. (1998). *Does it compute? The relationship between educational technology and student achievement in mathematics.* Princeton, NJ: Educational Testing Service.

Weschler, D. (1949). *Weschler intelligence scale for children: Manual.* New York: Psychological Corporation.

Where in the World Is Carmen Sandiego? (CD-ROM). (1995). Novato, CA: Broderbund Software.

Wolfe, P. (2001). *Brain matters: Translating research into classroom practice.* Alexandria, VA: Association for Supervision and Curriculum Development.

Wood, E., Willoughby, T., & Specht, J. (1998). What's happening with computer technology in early childhood education settings? *Journal of Educational Computing Research, 18*(3), 237–243.

Wright, J. L., & Shade, D. (Eds.). (1994). *Young children: Active learners in a technological age.* Washington, DC: National Association for the Education of Young Children.

Wright, J. L., & Thouvenelle, S. (1991). A developmental approach to teacher training. *Education and Computing: The International Journal, 7,* 223–229.

Index